BELOVED

CONTINUUM CHARACTER STUDIES

BELOVED
CHARACTER STUDIES

NANCY J. PETERSON

continuum

Continuum

The Tower Building
11 York Road
London SE1 7NX

80 Maiden Lane, Suite 704
New York
NY 10038

www.continuumbooks.com

First published 2008

British Library Cataloguing-in-Publication Data
A catalogue record for this book is available from the British Library.

ISBN: 978-0-8264-9574-7 (hardback)
978-0-8264-9575-4 (paperback)

Typeset by Servis Filmsetting Ltd, Manchester

CONTENTS

SERIES EDITOR'S PREFACE

This series aims to promote sophisticated literary analysis through the concept of character. It demonstrates the necessity of linking character analysis to texts' themes, issues and ideas, and encourages students to embrace the complexity of literary characters and the texts in which they appear. The series thus fosters close critical reading and evidence-based discussion, as well as an engagement with historical context, and with literary criticism and theory.

Character Studies was prompted by a general concern in literature departments about students responding to literary characters as if they were real people rather than fictional creations, and writing about them as if they were two-dimensional entities existing in an ahistorical space. Some students tend to think it is enough to observe that King Lear goes 'mad', that Frankenstein is 'ambitious', or that Vladimir and Estragon are 'tender and cruel'. Their comments are correct, but obviously limited.

Thomas Docherty, in his *Reading (Absent) Character: Towards a Theory of Characterization in Fiction*, reminds us to relate characters to ideas, but also stresses the necessity of engaging with the complexity of characters:

If we proceed with the same theory as we apply to allegory [that a character represents one thing, such as Obstinate in Bunyan's *Pilgrim's Progress*], then we will be led to accept that Madame Bovary 'means' or 'represents' some one essence or value, however complex that essence may be. But perhaps, and more likely, she is many things, and perhaps some of them lead to her character being incoherent, lacking unity, and so on . . . It is clearly wrong to say, in a critical reading, that Kurtz, for example, in Conrad's *Heart of Darkness* represents evil, or ambition, or any other one thing, and to leave it at that; nor is Jude a representative of 'failed aspirations' in Hardy's *Jude the Obscure*; nor is Heathcliff a representation of the proletariat in Emily Brontë's *Wuthering Heights*, and so on. There may be elements of truth in some of these readings of character, but the theory which rests content with trying to discover the singular simple essence of character in this way is inadequate. (1983, p. xii)

King Lear, for example, is complex, so not easily understandable, and is perhaps 'incoherent, lacking unity'; he is fictional, so must be treated as a construct; and he does not 'mean' or 'represent' one thing. We can relate him to ideas about power, control, judgement, value, sovereignty, the public and the private, sex and sexuality, the body, nature and nurture, appearance, inheritance, socialization, patriarchy, religion, will, blindness, sanity, violence, pessimism, hope, ageing, love, death, grief – and so on.

To ignore this, and to respond to Lear as if he is a real person talking ahistorically, means we simplify both the character and the play; it means, in short, that we forget our responsibilities as literary critics. When, for example, Lear cries, 'Howl, howl, howl, howl! O, you are men of stones!' (5.2.255), it would be wrong to ignore our emotional response, and to marginalize our empathy for a father carrying his dead daughter – but we must also engage with such other elements as: the meaning and repetition of 'Howl' (three howls in some editions, four in others); the uncertainty about to whom 'you are men of stones' is directed; what 'men of stones' meant to Shakespeare's audience; the various ways in which the line can be said, and the various effects produced; how what Lear says relates to certain issues in the play and introduces new ideas about being human; what literary critics have written about the line; and what literary theorists have said, or might say, about it.

When we embrace the complexity of character, when we

undertake detailed, sensitive critical analysis that acknowledges historical context, and literary criticism and theory, and when we relate characters to themes, issues and ideas, the texts we study blossom, beautifully and wonderfully, and we realize that we have so much more to say about them. We are also reminded of why they are worthy of study, of why they are important, of why they are great.

Ashley Chantler
University of Chester, UK

AN OVERVIEW OF *BELOVED*

In May 2006, A. O. Scott of the *New York Times Book Review* released the results of a request sent out to various literary critics, writers, and editors to name "the single best work of American fiction published in the last 25 years": Toni Morrison's 1987 novel, *Beloved*, received the most votes. Scott goes on to explain that "Any other outcome would have been startling, since Morrison's novel has inserted itself into the American canon more completely than any of its potential rivals." Why and how *Beloved* as a novel has come to command the interest and imagination of readers, students, teachers, and scholars, not only in the U.S.A. but worldwide, is a fascinating story in and of itself. The power of Morrison's lyrical language, her interest in reshaping American history while telling a gripping story about human lives under slavery, her depiction of African American men and women, her innovative narrative strategies – all these elements work together to make reading and analyzing *Beloved* a deeply engaging experience.

Toni Morrison was born on 18 February 1931 in Lorain, Ohio, a working-class town located about 25 miles west of Cleveland. The name on her birth certificate reads "Chloe Ardelia Wofford" (Duvall 2000, p. 42): the middle name, "Ardelia," honors her maternal grandmother, Ardelia Willis; her maiden name comes from her parents, Ramah and George Wofford. "Chloe," her given first name, eventually became the nickname "Toni," a shortened form of "Anthony" (derived from St. Anthony), the name Morrison chose for herself when she converted to Catholicism at age twelve. Her last name, "Morrison", comes from the Jamaican architect she was married to from 1958 to 1964, Harold Morrison. Knowing something of the various names Morrison has been identified with over the course of her lifetime provides a glimpse into the amazing development of her career.

Morrison's parents were originally from the South: her mother was born in Greenville, Alabama, her father in Cartersville, Georgia. Their families, as many other African Americans at the time did, migrated to the North to escape the violent racism of the South. George Wofford became a welder at U.S. Steel, but worked two or three jobs at a time to support his family. Morrison's mother was a homemaker for many years. Morrison's parents and grandparents loved singing, playing music, and storytelling. Morrison especially relished the ghost stories her mother told her, passed down from stories the family had told while still living in Alabama.

The Woffords struggled at times to make ends meet: during Morrison's childhood they lived in at least six different apartments in Lorain, one of which they fled when their landlord set it on fire because they couldn't pay the rent they owed him ($4 for the month). Her parents had very distinct views about the relationship between blacks and whites in America: her mother was hopeful whites could improve their moral fiber, but her father, as Morrison describes it, "distrust[ed] every word and every gesture of every white man on earth" (1976, p. 152).

Morrison was the only black child in her first grade classroom (Lorain schools were integrated), and she was the only one who had learned to read by the time she reached the first grade. She read voraciously growing up, especially classic British, American, French, and Russian novels, and the African American writers who were available to her at the time. She has commented that it was apparent early on to her family and to her teachers that she ought to get a substantial education. During her years at Lorain High School, Morrison was a member of the debating team, the yearbook staff, and the drama club. She chose to go to college at Howard University in Washington DC, where from 1949 to 1953 she earned her B.A. in English and a minor in Classics. She also joined the Howard University Players, a drama troupe that toured throughout the South; their travels sometimes resulted in an intimate understanding of Jim Crow segregation when they would arrive in a town too late to be accommodated in the "colored motel," as Morrison describes it (Als 2003, p. 68), and then would seek out assistance from local ministers to find a church basement or the floor of somebody's house to sleep on for the night. From Howard, Morrison went to Cornell University in Ithaca, New York, where she graduated in 1955 with an M.A. in American literature. Her master's thesis, exploring the theme of alienation in the works of Virginia Woolf and William Faulkner, has prompted scholars to link Morrison's novels to both Woolf's and (especially) Faulkner's fiction. She then did a short stint teaching at Texas Southern University in Houston, followed by a return to Howard, where she taught from 1957 to 1964. Also at this time, she joined a writing group and produced a short story that would later be developed into her first novel, *The Bluest Eye*.

While teaching at Howard, she met and married Harold Morrison, and they had two sons together: Harold Ford, born in 1961, and Slade Kevin, born in 1965, when Morrison had already divorced her husband. To support herself and her sons, Morrison went to work as a textbook editor at L. W. Singer (a division of Random House) based in Syracuse, New York. At night, after putting her sons in bed, Morrison worked on the manuscript for *The Bluest Eye*, which was initially turned down by several publishers, but finally was published in 1970 by Holt, Rinehart & Winston. In 1968, Morrison had moved to New York City to work as a Senior Editor in the scholastic division at Random House. Sometime after her first novel appeared, Morrison moved into the trade division, and she became an extraordinary editor of works by African American writers, intellectuals, and heroes during her years there. She capably and tirelessly promoted the work of Gayl Jones, June Jordan, Toni Cade (Bambara), Lucille Clifton, Angela Davis, Muhammad Ali, Henry Dumas, Leon Forrest, and many others. Morrison continued her work as an editor until 1983. She had already published four novels and was beginning to attract considerable attention from reviewers and scholars, and, in 1984, she accepted a position as the Albert Schweitzer Professor of the Humanities at the State University of New York at Albany, which allowed her to be a writer first and foremost. In 1989, Morrison became the Robert F. Goheen Professor in the Humanities at Princeton University in New Jersey, where she held a joint appointment in African American Studies and Creative Writing until she officially retired in 2006.

To date, Morrison has written and published eight novels, a book of literary criticism, seven children's books (six of them co-written with her son Slade), and is currently at work on a new novel, tentatively titled *Mercy*. She has also edited collections of essays on the Anita Hill-Clarence Thomas hearings and the O. J. Simpson case, written a play about the brutal lynching of Emmett Till, and the libretto for an opera based on *Beloved*.

Morrison's first novel, *The Bluest Eye*, is set close to home, in Lorain, Ohio, during the 1940s. It tells the story of two young black girls: Pecola Breedlove, who desperately wishes for blue eyes so that she can see herself as beautiful, and Claudia MacTeer, who tells her own story about what it is like to grow up black and female, showing how she learns to critique and resist negative images of blackness. Morrison's second novel, *Sula* (1973), spans the years from 1919 to 1965, following first the Peace family, then focusing on the young girl Sula Peace, who develops into an out-of-bounds adult black woman, whose independent lifestyle shocks the black community and even her own best friend from childhood, Nel Wright.

Morrison's first two novels resulted in steadily growing recognition, but her third novel, *Song of Solomon* (1977), made her nationally known. The novel tells the story of the Dead family: Macon and his wife, Ruth; their three children, First Corinthians, Lena, and Milkman; and Macon's estranged sister, Pilate, along with her daughter, Reba, and granddaughter, Hagar. The novel is a coming-of-age story, focusing on Milkman's attempt to become his own individual, which involves learning what to reject and what to accept of his friends" and family's influences. *Song of Solomon* was named a Book of the Month Club selection, the first book by an African American author to receive such an endorsement since Richard Wright's *Native Son* in 1940; it also won the National Book Critics Circle Award and became a bestseller in paperback.

Tar Baby (1981) was also published to acclaim, and remained on the *New York Times* bestseller list for four months. In fact, *Newsweek* featured Morrison on the cover of the 30 March 1981 issue: she was the first African American woman to be on the cover of a national news magazine in the U.S.A. since Zora Neale Hurston in 1943. Perhaps it is no accident that the critical establishment, dominated by white reviewers and editors, was so enthusiastic about this novel in particular, for unlike the novels that precede it, *Tar Baby* is set in the Caribbean and features two white characters (Valerian and Margaret Street) along with two central black protagonists – Son, a young vibrant male who is steeped in indigenous folk culture, and Jadine, a beautiful woman who identifies with modernity, cosmopolitanism, and independence.

It was the publication of *Beloved* in 1987 that brought Morrison to the forefront of American letters. The novel made the *New York Times* bestseller list the week it was published, and three weeks later, it had climbed to the number three spot on that list. The initial print run for the book was 100,000 copies, but at the end of the first month, the novel was already in its third printing. Walter Clemons's assessment of the novel for *Newsweek* – "I think we have a masterpiece on our hands here" (p. 75) – indicates the overwhelming response to Morrison's novel that many readers and reviewers expressed (more about this response below). *Beloved* at its core is a novel about Sethe, a slave mother who loves her children so much she would rather kill them than see them returned to slavery, and Beloved, the daughter who is killed and who then returns to haunt the family, first as ghost, then in the flesh. But the novel is also about how to reconstruct one's self as free in the aftermath of slavery as trauma. To that end, the novel moves back and forth between two time frames: 1855, when Sethe and her children flee Sweet Home, Kentucky, and 1873, when one of the former slaves from Sweet Home, Paul D, shows up at Sethe's house on the outskirts of Cincinnati, Ohio.

As scholar Marilyn Sanders Mobley points out, "Although the relevance of history informs all of her [Morrison's] novels from *The Bluest Eye* to *Tar Baby*, it is in *Beloved* that history simultaneously becomes both theme and narrative process" (p. 357).

5

Morrison's early novels, while set within significant historical eras, tend to emphasize folklore and the mythic dimensions of black life. *Beloved*, however, is the first volume of a historical trilogy, including *Jazz* (1992) and *Paradise* (1998), and marks a shift in Morrison's focus toward rewriting African American History as history – as the story of individual black men and women seeking to create a "livable life" (1987b, p. 234) out of their personal, historical, and social circumstances. As mentioned above, *Beloved*, set in 1873 but flashing back to 1855, explores lives frayed by slavery. *Jazz*, set in the 1920s in New York City, focuses on Joe and Violet Trace, who have migrated from the South to the North during the years when the Jazz Age and the Harlem Renaissance made it possible to be a "New Negro," as Alain Locke termed it (p. 3). But all this change cuts off Joe and Violet from something vital, and the novel follows their loss of self and community, Joe's affair with another woman, and the couple's struggle to find their way back to one other. *Paradise*, the culminating novel of the trilogy, is set in an all-black town in Oklahoma during the 1970s and focuses on two communities opposed to each other: the town of Ruby, where safety and order are maintained through insularity, pure bloodlines, and patriarchal authority, and the Convent, a community of wayward women trying to live according to their own desires and ethos.

Since the completion of her trilogy, Morrison has published a novel entitled *Love* (2003), which features Bill Cosey, a black entrepreneur in a Jim Crow era, who is both magnificent and oppressive. The novel traces his continuing influence on the lives of the present-day characters, long after his death. The title of Morrison's 2003 novel directly points to an abiding theme that runs throughout her novels, the risks and blessings of love – of loving oneself, of loving another, of loving too much, of failing to love wisely or deeply. In fact, in a 1985 interview with novelist Gloria Naylor, Morrison indicated that the theme of love is the connective tissue for what would become her historical trilogy. She told Naylor that Margaret Garner's decision to kill her children to keep them out of slavery, the historical incident that inspired *Beloved* (discussed in detail in the following chapter), became intertwined for her with the story behind a funereal photograph of a young black woman, beautifully dressed and coiffed, resting in a satin-lined coffin. This photograph, taken by the acclaimed African American photographer James Van Der Zee in 1926 and reprinted in a volume called *The Harlem Book of the Dead* (1978), became the inspiration for *Jazz*. Van Der Zee's woman had been shot by her former lover at a party, but did not tell anyone of the shooting, and the people surrounding her noticed only when she collapsed that she was bleeding. She refused medical treatment and refused to summon the police, evidently in order to let her lover escape, and so she died. In both of these stories, Morrison explains to Naylor, "A woman loved something other than herself so much. She had placed all of the value of her life in something outside herself" (1985, p. 207). Morrison goes on to clarify this theme:

> Now both of those incidents seem to me, at least on the surface, very noble, you know, in that old-fashioned sense, noble things, generous, wide-spirited, love beyond the call. . . . It's peculiar to women. And I thought, it's interesting because the best thing that is in us is also the thing that makes us sabotage ourselves, sabotage in the sense that our life is not as worthy, or our perception of the best part of ourselves. (1985, p. 208)

Morrison's comments clearly raise important tensions that emerge in *Beloved*.

The theme of love, however, was not typically discussed in the many reviews of the novel that appeared after it was published in September 1987. In fact, the early reviews demonstrate the novel's ability both to impress and confound readers. Some reviewers raved about the brilliance of the novel; some were even-handed in their assessment, pointing to both strengths and weaknesses; a few others were harshly critical. Margaret Atwood and A. S. Byatt, both acclaimed authors themselves, found the novel to be groundbreaking and original. Atwood's review appeared just as the novel was released, and Atwood did not hesitate to position *Beloved* at the pinnacle of Morrison's career: "Morrison's versatility and technical and emotional range appear to know no bounds. If there were any doubts about her stature as a pre-eminent American novelist, of her own or any other generation, *Beloved* will put them to rest" (p. 39). Byatt, likewise, pronounced the novel "an American masterpiece" and compared it favorably to the works of canonical American writers of the nineteenth century. She writes at the end of her review that *Beloved*

> in a curious way[,] reassesses all the major novels of the time in which it is set. Melville, Hawthorne, Poe, wrote riddling allegories about the nature of evil, the haunting of unappeased spirits, the inverted opposition of blackness and whiteness. Toni Morrison has with plainness and grace and terror – and judgment – solved the riddle, and showed us the world which haunted theirs. (p. 13)

Atwood too singled out the depiction of ghosts in the novel as remarkable and compared Morrison's novel to another classic: "The supernatural element is treated, not in an 'Amityville Horror', watch-me-make-your-flesh-creep mode, but with magnificent practicality, like the ghost of Catherine Earnshaw in *Wuthering Heights*" (p. 40).

Atwood and Byatt also found Morrison's depiction of slavery to be brilliantly eye-opening. In her comments, Atwood emphasizes the unflinching treatment of the brutalities of slavery:

> [W]e experience American slavery as it was lived by those who were its objects of exchange, both at its best – which wasn't very good – and at its worst, which was as bad as can be imagined. Above all, it is seen as one of the most viciously anti-family institutions human beings have ever devised. The slaves are motherless, fatherless, deprived of their mates, their children, their kin. It is a world in which people suddenly vanish and are never seen again, not through accident or covert operation or terrorism, but as a matter of everyday legal policy. (pp. 40–1)

While Atwood's description points to the outrageous horror of slavery as depicted in Morrison's novel, Byatt comments insightfully about Morrison's careful balancing of the degradations of slavery and the humanity of the slaves. "The slaves whose stories lie behind Toni Morrison's novel were thought by whites at this time to be in some way animal. The case for slavery was argued on these grounds," Byatt explains, and then adds: "What Toni Morrison does is present an image of a people so wholly human that they are almost superhuman. It is a magnificent achievement" (p. 13).

One other element of *Beloved* that both Atwood and Byatt commend is Morrison's prose style. Byatt says she found herself mesmerized by "the exact beauty of the singing prose" (p. 13), while Atwood describes the language of the novel as "rich, graceful, eccentric, rough, lyrical, sinuous, colloquial and very much to the point" (p. 42). Both reviewers note that Morrison's dazzling language is vital for narrating the difficult history the novel explores and for making the supernatural elements of the story believable.

Morrison's novel immediately impressed both Byatt and Atwood as being among the most compelling contemporary novels. Other reviewers were not so sure. Judith Thurman, writing for the *New Yorker*, found the novel effective in "driv[ing] home the meaning of slavery" (p. 179), but also subject to "occasional excesses of rhetoric (and sentimentality)" (p. 177). Nonetheless, she concludes her review by endorsing the novel: "But if you read *Beloved* with a vigilant eye, you should also listen to it with a vigilant ear. There's something great in it: a play of human voices, consciously exalted, perversely stressed, yet holding true. It gets you" (p. 180). Ann Snitow, reviewing the novel for the *Village Voice*, also admired Morrison's method of telling the story:

> Told flat, the plot of *Beloved* is the stuff of melodrama, recalling *Uncle Tom's Cabin*. But Morrison doesn't really *tell* these incidents. Bits and pieces of them leak out between the closed eyelids of her characters, or between their clenched fingers. She twists and tortures and fractures events until they are little slivers that cut. She moves the lurid material of melodrama into the minds of her people, where it gets sifted and sorted, lived and relived, until it acquires the enlarging outlines of myth and trauma, dream and obsession. (p. 48)

This is high praise indeed, but Snitow ultimately argues that the novel "fails in its ambitions" (p. 50). She finds the depiction of Beloved as ghost unconvincing and not capable of carrying the "weight of meaning" the novel attributes to her (p. 50). Snitow also sees the culmination of the romance plot (bringing Paul D and Sethe back together at the end) as coming close to being a pat happy ending, even as she also commends the very last section of the novel – the coda – for its lyricism and poignancy.

Like Snitow's review, Rosellen Brown's evaluation of *Beloved* for the *Nation* points to what she describes as "a slightly uneven, stepping-stone quality" (p. 62). And like Snitow, Brown distrusts the happy ending:

> In some profound way I believe in the beauty and horror of the individual instances more than I do in the story, in which a mother who has felt herself guilty of an atrocity for nearly two decades finally makes peace with herself and begins a "new" life with a man who has never stopped being good, no matter what has happened to undo him. The will to console, to make a positive myth out of unspeakable circumstances, seems to have moved Morrison to wrench her characters nearly free of their ghosts when we might imagine them fighting to a more complex or ambivalent conclusion. (pp. 62–3)

Despite this flaw and others, Brown deemed *Beloved* to be "an extraordinary novel" (p. 59) because of its stunning language and black speech rhythms, because of its depiction of Beloved as both ghost and body, and because of its treatment of memory and psychology.

It is important to consider carefully what elements reviewers highlighted in their commentary at the time when *Beloved* was published: even though the novel sprang from a specific historical incident, there were no immediate precedents for a novel like *Beloved*, in terms of American literary history or in the context of Morrison's career. Although some reviewers of the novel when it first appeared tried to make connections to what was already familiar (Morrison's preceding novels, classic American novels, and so on), such comparisons were not always fair or insightful.

Other reviewers clearly did not know what to make of *Beloved*. Stanley Crouch, writing for the *New Republic*, for example, declared *Beloved* to be marred by a black feminist slant that vilifies black men. Crouch also judged the novel to be completely unconvincing in its depiction of slavery; in fact, he describes *Beloved* as "a blackface holocaust novel . . . written in order to enter American slavery into the big-time martyr ratings contest, a contest usually won by references to, and works about, the experience of Jews at the hands of Nazis" (p. 40). In biting sarcasm, Crouch suggests in his review that Morrison wrote a sentimental, melodramatic novel that could easily be adapted as a successful television soap opera or mini-series because of its obvious and trite treatment of what should be epic tragedy. Looking back at Crouch's review, readers and scholars today can detect Crouch's uneasiness with the flourishing literary production of black female authors at the time, in novels that often challenged some of the orthodoxies of what African American male writers had been saying in their work. Crouch also seems quick to place *Beloved* in the midst of heated debates of the 1980s about how to account for downward mobility among black people in America, and he specifically sees Morrison's novel as emphasizing a social determinism that does not pay enough attention to individual responsibility. But should the concerns of the 1980s be brought to bear so heavily on a novel set in 1873?

One of the other staunchly critical reviews of *Beloved* was written by Carol Iannone and published in *Commentary*. As her title – "Toni Morrison's Career" – suggests, Iannone approaches *Beloved* via a discussion of the novels Morrison published leading up to it. This perspective allows her to recognize "many compelling elements" in the novel, while also judging *Beloved* to be "far from successful as a work of art" (p. 63). Like Crouch, Iannone is troubled by the novel's emphasis on the horrors of slavery:

[T]he book grows massive and heavy with cumulative and oft-repeated miseries, with new miseries and new dimensions of miseries added in each telling and retelling long after the point has been made and the reader has grown numb. The graphic descriptions of physical humiliation begin to grow sensationalistic, and the gradual unfolding of secret horror has an unmistakably Gothic dimension which soon comes to seem merely lurid, designed to arouse and entertain. (p. 63)

For Iannone, the brutalities of slavery depicted in *Beloved* are first too repetitious, then too titillating.

In sharp contrast to Iannone's and Crouch's contentions that the horrific depiction of slavery in *Beloved* is meant to entertain readers, Morrison confessed to interviewer Bonnie Angelo that she did not expect the novel to be successful at all:

> I thought this has got to be the least read of all the books I'd written because it is about something that the characters don't want to remember, I don't want to remember, black people don't want to remember, white people don't want to remember. I mean, it's national amnesia. (1989c, p. 257)

Reviewers who ultimately endorsed the novel appreciated *Beloved*'s ambition to call attention to this national amnesia – not only by telling the story of slavery in such harrowing detail, but by revealing parts of the story that are lost or so traumatic that they require innovative language and techniques to render their ineffability. In an interview with Marsha Darling, Morrison emphasizes the role of the reader in making her stories compelling:

> It's very important . . . that the writing be as understated and as quiet as possible, and as clean as possible and as lean as possible in order to make a complex and rich response come from the reader.
>
> They always say that my writing is rich. It's not – what's rich, if there is any richness, is what the reader gets and brings him or herself. That's part of the way in which the tale is told. The folk tales are told in such a way that whoever is listening is in it and can shape it and figure it out. (1988, p. 253)

In Morrison's perspective, readers are called to the novel to bring themselves and their imaginations to bear in order to make the stories emerge in all their richness and complexity. What readers –

and reviewers – bring to the experience of reading *Beloved* ultimately influences their appreciation or condemnation of the novel.

At the time of its publication, *Beloved* became the site of a controversy about the awarding of prestigious literary prizes and whether the critical establishment deemed novels focusing on African American lives, written by African Americans, worthy of these prizes. In fall of 1987, *Beloved* was passed over for the National Book Award for Fiction (*Paco's Story* by Larry Heinemann won) and for the National Book Critics Circle Award for Fiction (which went to Philip Roth's *The Counterlife*), and African American writer James Baldwin died on 30 November 1987 without being recognized by either the National Book Award or a Pulitzer Prize during his lifetime. Leading African American intellectuals were outraged, and they wrote an open letter calling attention to this critical neglect that was published in the *New York Times Book Review* on 24 January 1988. The opening statement, written by June Jordan and Houston A. Baker Jr., riffed on the theme of the beloved from Morrison's novel and then discussed Baldwin and Morrison as two legendary writers who experienced critical neglect. The opening section was followed by a tribute to Morrison signed by 48 African American scholars and writers, not only to protest the failure of the major award committees to recognize any of Morrison's novels, but to pay tribute to the writer and her imaginative vision:

> Alive, we write this testament of thanks to you, dear Toni: alive, beloved and persevering, magical. . . . You have never turned away the searching eye, the listening ear attuned to horror or to histories providing for our faith. And freely you have given to us every word that you have found important to the forward movement of our literature, our life. For all of America, for all of American letters, you have advanced the moral and artistic standards by which we must measure the daring and the love of our national imagination and our collective intelligence as a people.

This very public pronouncement significantly positioned Morrison as a writer "for all of America," even as her works focus on the "collective intelligence" of African Americans. On 1 April 1988 came the public announcement that Morrison's *Beloved* had been awarded the Pulitzer Prize for Fiction.

Five years later, in December 1993, Morrison's literary and critical work was recognized with the most prestigious prize worldwide for "word-work" (as she called it in her acceptance speech), when Morrison became the ninetieth laureate (but the first African American) writer to win the Nobel Prize in Literature. In announcing the award on 7 October 1993, the Swedish Academy mentioned three of Morrison's novels specifically – *Song of Solomon*, *Beloved*, and *Jazz* – and commended Morrison as a writer, "who, in novels characterized by visionary force and poetic import, gives life to an essential aspect of American reality." Yet the award was not without controversy. African American writer Charles Johnson, who won the 1990 National Book Award for his powerful novel *The Middle Passage*, responded to the announcement of Morrison's award by saying it "was a triumph of political correctness," and Stanley Crouch, who wrote a vituperative review of *Beloved* (discussed above), commented, "I hope this prize inspires her to write better books" (Streitfeld 1993, p. A16).

What has become clear in the years since Morrison won the Nobel Prize is that she is *the* contemporary American author to be reckoned with. The historical trilogy that began with *Beloved*, then moved to *Jazz*, and culminated in *Paradise*, continues to be taught, analyzed, and debated (and sometimes banned) in classrooms across the U.S.A. and around the world. Scholars have found *Beloved* as a novel intriguing and valuable for asking questions from a variety of disciplinary perspectives, including African American studies, literary studies, American studies, women's studies, and postcolonial studies. *Beloved* still occupies a superlative position in Morrison's oeuvre; its relentless and lyrical investigation of the essential questions and conundrums surrounding freedom, selfhood, love, and responsibility are timeless and elusive. So gripping are the story and themes found in *Beloved* that Morrison collaborated with the composer Richard Danielpour to create an opera based on it: titled *Margaret Garner*, the opera premiered in May 2005 at the Michigan Opera Theatre in Detroit.

Many of the questions raised by reviewers and commentators on *Beloved* will be explored in depth in the following chapters. The purpose of this guide to *Beloved* is to tease out a sophisticated analysis of the novel by focusing specifically on the characters. The first chapter explores the novel's links to history, explaining the Margaret Garner case that Morrison drew on as well as other historical influences that shaped the novel. Chapter 2 focuses on black mothers and daughters in the novel, outlining how slavery perverted and twisted motherhood and mothering for black women, and how Morrison's characters, such as Sethe, Denver, and Baby Suggs, develop strategies to resist those effects. Chapter 3 concentrates on the central enigma of the novel, the character of Beloved, who is both ghost and flesh and who comes to symbolize a range of interpretive meanings. Black men and their conceptions of manhood are the focus of Chapter 4; close analyses of Sixo, Halle, Stamp Paid, and Paul D suggest the various ways slavery impacted selfhood and identity for these men. The final chapter turns to the representation of white characters (whom Morrison calls "whitefolks," rendered as one word) and ideologies of whiteness in the novel, demonstrating that race by itself does not determine the decency or depravity of Morrison's characters. A brief conclusion links the character analyses carried out in the various chapters to the most significant themes and issues of *Beloved*.

Throughout this study, page references to *Beloved* are to the paperback edition of the novel published by Vintage Books (a division of Random House) in 2004. This edition of the novel is especially noteworthy, for it includes a new foreword written by Morrison that talks about some of the issues and difficulties she faced while working on the novel. Her foreword, followed by the text of the novel itself, sets readers on a journey into the minds and hearts of Morrison's unforgettable characters, who are the center of attention in the chapters that follow.

CHAPTER 1

HISTORY AND *BELOVED*

The opening scene of *Beloved* takes place in 1873 during the summer, when Sethe returns home to find Paul D, someone she has not seen or heard from since she fled Sweet Home and slavery 18 years earlier, sitting on the porch of her house. The present time action of the novel continues from 1873 into 1874, when the novel ends with Beloved's disappearance and Sethe's reconnection to the black community. While the novel's action takes place during 1873–74, which falls into the Reconstruction Era of U.S. history, much of the narration concerns a period of time from the 1850s leading up to 1855, when the slaves of Sweet Home, a plantation located in Kentucky, attempt to escape to Ohio to gain their freedom. So powerful are these stories from the past that *Beloved* is often referred to as a novel about slavery, or in Bernard Bell's term, a "neo-slave narrative" (p. 9), when in fact the novel begins almost 20 years later. Analyzing the historical setting of *Beloved* alongside the actual historical case that inspired the novel provides valuable insights into Morrison's purposes.

Morrison's idea for the novel was sparked by a particular historical incident: on the night of 27 January 1856, Margaret and Robert Garner, along with their four children and Robert's parents, fled from their respective plantations in Boone County, Kentucky. Using a stolen sleigh and a team of horses, they travelled approximately 18 miles north from Richwood to Covington in Kentucky; then they abandoned the sleigh and crossed the frozen Ohio River on foot, taking refuge at the Cincinnati home of Margaret's kin, Joe and Elijah Kite, who had been freed from slavery. On the morning of 28 January 1856, while the family awaited instructions from Levi Coffin, a well-known Quaker abolitionist, they were surrounded by a group of slave catchers, including U.S. marshals, Archibald Gaines (Margaret's owner and the master of Maplewood), and the son of Robert's owner. While the posse entered the house, Robert shot at them before his pistol was taken away. At the same time, Margaret tried to kill all four of her children, but succeeded in killing only one: Mary, two years old, who was described by newspapers of the time and in court testimony as being almost white in skin color. Margaret had grabbed a butcher's knife and slit her daughter's throat from ear to ear, almost severing her head from her body. Explaining her desperate actions directed toward her children, Margaret said that she "would much rather kill them at once, and thus end their sufferings, than have them taken back to slavery and be murdered by piecemeal" (Gordon 1997, p. 157).

The Margaret Garner story had several twists and turns as it unfolded. Bystanders at the scene on 28 January 1856 described Archibald Gaines as emerging from the house in tears, holding Mary's dead body – an unusual reaction, perhaps signaling that he, not Margaret's husband, had fathered the girl. Later that day, he took the girl's body with him back to Kentucky to bury her at Maplewood, another unprecedented action for a white master to perform for a slave child. Subsequent commentators have wondered if Margaret specifically chose that child to kill as a means of striking back at her master in a most effective way. Steven Weisenburger, the scholar who has studied the historical case more extensively than anyone else, observes:

> As for the infanticide, what *had* Margaret Garner done? Destroyed her master's *property* with the same knife stroke that destroyed his *progeny* (if Gaines fathered Mary Garner). On this view of things, Margaret's child-murder was a masterstroke of rebellion against the whole patriarchal system of American slavery. (pp. 77–8)

Certainly it is the case that the legal system was baffled by what crime Margaret Garner should be charged with. Was she subject to the Fugitive Slave Law of 1850, under which slaves like the Garners who fled and escaped to free states like Ohio could be recaptured and remanded to their masters? Or should Margaret be charged with the murder of her child? To charge her with murder, however, Margaret would have to be considered to possess legal personhood, a difficult proposition given the ideology of slavery that extended even into the city of Cincinnati, located in the free state of Ohio. Moreover, the legal intricacies of the case pitted U.S. federal statutes, in the form of the Fugitive Slave Law, against states" rights – in this case, the right of Ohio as a free state to charge Margaret with murder. Weisenburger aptly describes the legal conundrum in the following way: "Could federal law force Ohio to give up alleged felons because Kentucky law said they were also property? Even when Ohio law expressly prohibited property in human beings? More generally, did constitutional protections of property take precedence over human rights?" (p. 112). Abolitionists of the time advocated and advised Margaret to accept the murder charge, if it became possible, because it would allow her to remain in Ohio and would also give them time to try to purchase her and her children from Gaines if need be.

First came the ruling that Margaret was subject to the Fugitive Slave Law, which allowed Archibald Gaines to reclaim her and the children and take them to Kentucky. Margaret's lawyers and fellow abolitionists did not give up, however, and just when it looked as though they might succeed in having Margaret returned to Ohio to stand trial on the murder charge, Gaines shipped Margaret and her family down the Mississippi River to a plantation further south. On that journey in March 1856, their steamboat collided with another boat, almost cutting theirs in half and starting a fire below deck. Accounts of the time do not reveal all the facts: it is not clear if the force of the accident itself threw Margaret and baby Cilla into the water or if Margaret herself threw the baby into the water and tried to follow. But the end result was that baby Cilla drowned, while Margaret was rescued. Margaret eventually ended up working on a plantation in Mississippi, where in 1858 she died of typhoid fever.

Robert Garner and his two sons survived slavery. In fact, Robert fought in the Civil War, and after the war ended, he moved to a small farm outside of Vicksburg, Mississippi, where he raised Thomas and Samuel. In 1870, Robert was interviewed by a *Cincinnati Chronicle* reporter, who stated that Robert had remarried and was currently living in the city of Cincinnati. Where and when he died remains unclear.

Although this is the historical incident that Toni Morrison drew on for *Beloved*, Morrison did not have access to all these details when she worked on her novel. Morrison became aware of the Margaret Garner case as she worked with Middleton Harris on assembling *The Black Book* in the 1970s, when she was a senior editor at Random House. *The Black Book* resembles a scrapbook: it includes newspaper clippings, photographs and sketches, recipes, songs and poems, sheet music, advertisements, and a wealth of other materials. It is designed to collect and remember black folklore, collective knowledge, and history, or "Black Life as lived", as Morrison describes it in an essay (1974, p. 89). On page 10 of *The Black Book* is an article from the *American Baptist* newspaper, written by the Reverend P. C. Bassett, titled "A Visit to the Slave Mother Who Killed Her Child." This clipping includes the essential facts of the case: that Margaret killed her two-year-old baby girl by slitting her throat, that she calmly stated that she had wanted to kill all her children to save them from slavery, and that abolitionists of the time had taken up her cause, hoping to use the circumstances to overturn the Fugitive Slave Law.

While Morrison knew the basic outline of the Margaret Garner case, she has indicated to several interviewers that she did not want to know too many details. "I did research about a lot of things in this book in order to narrow it, to make it narrow and deep," Morrison explained to Marsha Darling, "but I did not do much research on Margaret Garner other than the obvious stuff, because I wanted to invent her life" (1988, p. 248). While keeping to the central story involving Margaret Garner and the killing of her two-year-old daughter, Morrison makes liberal changes in names, dates, details, and narrative outcomes. The historical Margaret and Mary Garner become Sethe and Beloved in Morrison's novel, Cilla becomes Denver, and Mary (Robert's mother) becomes Baby Suggs. Although the escape originally happened in the thick of winter, in Morrison's novel it happens in summer, when the corn is high at Sweet Home. The historical Margaret and Robert Garner did not have the same owners and therefore did not see each other very often; in Morrison's novel, Sethe and Halle are both located at Sweet Home, which is run by the Garner family, not the Gaines family as in the historical incident. Furthermore, in Morrison's novel, all of Sethe's children are fathered by Halle; the historical Margaret Garner, however, had four children of varying skin tones, indicating that her husband likely was not the father of all of them. In the historical incident, the whole family – Margaret, Robert, their four children, and his parents – escape together, while in Morrison's novel, Baby Suggs is purchased and moves to Cincinnati well before the escape attempt, and Halle apparently never gets away from Sweet Home to join his family in Ohio. Perhaps most importantly, Morrison changes the outcome of Margaret Garner's story: she imagines Sethe in 1873 living on the outskirts of Cincinnati as a free black woman with her remaining daughter; in contrast, the historical Margaret Garner spent much of her time after the escape attempt and Mary's death either in jail, being used as a pawn by Archibald Gaines in various legal games, or doing hard labor at the plantation in Mississippi, where her life ended in 1858.

While Margaret Garner's case was the initial impetus for the novel, it is also clear that Morrison's interest in the material stemmed from a broader commitment to break the many silences surrounding slavery. In "A Bench by the Road," Morrison eloquently explains her sense of how *Beloved* might memorialize slavery and the millions of Africans and African Americans who suffered under it:

> There is no place you or I can go, to think about or not think about, to summon the presences of, or recollect the absences of slaves; nothing that reminds us of the ones who made the journey and of those who did not make it. There is no suitable memorial or plaque or wreath or wall or park or skyscraper lobby. There's no 300-foot tower. There's no small bench by the road. There is not even a tree scored, an initial that I can

visit or you can visit in Charleston or Savannah or New York or Providence or, better still, on the banks of the Mississippi. And because such a place doesn't exist (that I know of), the book had to. (1989a, p. 4)

Morrison's eloquence makes clear the kind of national amnesia that surrounds slavery in the United States. Official documents of the slave era were typically written by white ship captains, white traders, and white owners, who were interested primarily in recording their attempts to make a profit on their so-called investment. These historical documents, of course, do not reveal the perspectives of black people suffering and struggling to endure the slave system. Trying to recover this unwritten aspect of history is difficult, if not impossible: how can something that has never been recorded be remembered? And even if that were possible, how many white Americans even today are willing to remember and reckon with an era that was so ignoble and inhumane? Into this space of national absence and amnesia, Morrison inserts her novel as a memorial to honor and mourn all those who lived in, died from, suffered, and endured the slave system.

It is also important to recall that, during the nineteenth century, African Americans wrote slave narratives to create a counterdiscourse to the official documents of slaveowners and their specious claims about the benevolence of the institution. In a well-known essay titled "The Site of Memory," written while she was working on *Beloved*, Morrison talks about slave narratives and how important they are as a genre in African American literary history. She notes how *Beloved* draws on this tradition, but she also shows the need for her novel to break certain kinds of silences found in these narratives. Referring to slave narratives written by Olaudah Equiano, Frederick Douglass, Harriet Jacobs, and Henry Bibb, Morrison first identifies two key elements found in all of them:

One: "This is my historical life – my singular, special example that is personal, but that also represents the race". Two: "I write this text to persuade other people – you, the reader, who is probably not black – that we are human beings worthy of

God's grace and the immediate abandonment of slavery".
(1987a, pp. 104–5)

These were the conventions of the genre that allowed slave narratives to be read as credible to sympathetic white readers of the time. Morrison, however, points out that typically the slave's narrative was not sufficient on its own: abolitionists routinely surrounded the narrative with testimonials and letters from well-known whites to corroborate it. Morrison's novel, in contrast to this kind of authenticating apparatus, puts black characters at the center and moves white characters, some of whom are abolitionists, well to the margins.

In the essay, Morrison also goes on to point out several aspects of slavery that narratives of the nineteenth century were not able to describe openly. She discusses the fact that slaves were not allowed to react strongly or emotionally to tragic events or acts of cruelty in their narratives; objectivity was required to underscore the narrative as factual, and "there was no mention of their interior life" (1987a, pp. 106, 110). Unlike the objectivity found in nineteenth-century narratives, *Beloved* explores the traumatic crises caused by slavery and the devastating psychological effects that linger years later. To develop this interior view, Morrison creates a narrative that constantly drifts from present to past and back again, as bits and pieces of memories float to the surface, then sink to the bottom, perhaps to be recalled more fully the next time. She also infuses the language of the novel with vivid, sometimes startling images that speak to her characters" innermost needs, losses, and desires. At times, in fact, it feels as though readers are privy to aspects of interior life that remain unconscious to the characters themselves, as when the interior voices of Sethe, Denver, and Beloved merge in a kind of trialogue in Part Two of the novel (see pp. 256–8).

Another aspect of nineteenth-century slave narratives that *Beloved* dares to breach is the silence about the harrowing brutalities of slavery. Morrison explains:

[P]opular taste discouraged the writers from dwelling too long or too carefully on the more sordid details of their experience.

Whenever there was an unusually violent incident, or a scato-logical one, or something "excessive", one finds the writer taking refuge in the literary conventions of the day. . . . In shaping the experience to make it palatable to those who were in a position to alleviate it, they were silent about many things, and they "forgot" many other things. (1987a, pp. 109–10)

Morrison goes on to add that her "job" as a "writer in the last quarter of the twentieth century, not much more than a hundred years after Emancipation, a writer who is black and a woman" is "to rip that veil drawn over 'proceedings too terrible to related'" (1987a, p. 110). As mentioned in the Introduction to this guide, many reviewers commented on this aspect of Morrison's novel, most admiring Morrison's efforts to expose the myriad kinds of violence slavery inflicted. *Beloved* does not flinch when it comes to discussing whippings (think of the intricate pattern of scars on Sethe's back), lynchings, and the disciplinary equipment of slavery – the chains, the spoked collar that subjects Paul D to utter humiliation, the bit that Sethe's ma'am is forced to wear so often that her mouth permanently curves upward as if in a smile.

Morrison also reveals in *Beloved* the sexual exploitation that was a large part of the terror of slavery for black women. As Harriet Jacobs laments in her 1861 slave narrative, "Slavery is ter-rible for men; but it is far more terrible for women" (p. 77). Morrison's novel shows clearly why this is the case: Sethe is "milked" by schoolteacher's nephews; Baby Suggs's eight chil-dren have six different fathers; Ella recalls her sexual captivity by a white father and son, whom she thinks of as "the lowest yet" (p. 301).

What was silenced or forgotten in slave narratives of the nine-teenth century has often remained unremembered and unspoken into the twentieth century. This kind of critical absence or national amnesia is found not only in white dominant America, but in the oral traditions of the black community as well, as Morrison indicates in an interview:

I think Afro-Americans in rushing away from slavery, which was important to do – it meant rushing out of bondage into freedom – also rushed away from the slaves because it was painful to dwell there, and they may have abandoned some responsibilities in so doing. (1988, p. 247)

Barbara Christian makes a similar point in a 1990 essay tellingly titled "'Somebody Forget to Tell Somebody Something': African-American Women's Historical Novels," when she observes that upwardly mobile African Americans of the 1940s and 1950s did not want to pass down stories of enslavement, dispossession, and despair to their children, but thus left holes in their understanding of African American history that contemporary novels such as *Beloved* attempt to redress (pp. 326–7). In *Beloved*, Morrison thematizes the unwillingness of the community to confront the past directly in two significant ways. First, by having the events of 18 years earlier result in an unrelenting standoff between Sethe and her neighbors, the novel underscores that no one wants to think about the day when the community offered no warning of schoolteacher's ride toward 124 Bluestone Road. Second, in the final pages of the novel, the narrative voice reflects on how quickly Beloved is forgotten: "Disremembered and unaccounted for, she cannot be lost because no one is looking for her" (p. 323). No one desires to claim her or to claim memory of the trauma she represents.

If neither history, slave narratives, nor oral traditions are entirely trustworthy or accurate when trying to understand slavery, then what can Morrison do as a novelist to fill the gaps or call attention to what is missing? The power of Morrison's novel lies not only in her commitment to reveal aspects of slavery that had previously been unspeakable or unspoken (to cite key terms from the title of her eloquent 1989 essay), but also in the way that it dramatizes the difficulties and risks of remembering. As mentioned above, the novel takes place 18 years after Sethe fled Sweet Home and ended up killing her beloved daughter, and it is set almost a decade after the end of slavery and the truce of the Civil War. Why does slavery then haunt the characters' lives as though it were still potent and present? As Sally Keenan suggests, Morrison's decision to set the novel in 1873 is significant:

[Morrison] situates her characters in the Reconstruction period, when the institution of slavery was finally beginning to crumble, thus locating them at a crucial juncture both historically and psychologically between enslavement and emancipation. They are ... physically and notionally free but not psychologically free. They have just managed to escape from the fact of slavery but have not been released from its effects. (pp. 49–50)

What becomes clear as the novel unfolds is that some incidents for Sethe and Paul D have been so traumatic that they cannot bear to, or they essentially are unable to, remember them. Even years later, these memories result in overwhelming anguish, as though the experience were being repeated in the present. This is the dangerous aspect of "rememory" that Sethe tells Denver of early in the novel:

Someday you be walking down the road and you hear something or see something going on. So clear. And you think it's you thinking it up. A thought picture. But no. It's when you bump into a rememory that belongs to somebody else. Where I was before I came here, that place is real. It's never going away. Even if the whole farm – every tree and grass blade of it dies. The picture is still there and what's more, if you go there – you who never was there – if you go there and stand in the place where it was, it will happen again; it will be there for you, waiting for you. So, Denver, you can't never go there. Never. Because even though it's all over – over and done with – it's going to always be there waiting for you. (pp. 43–4)

As Mae G. Henderson has observed, in Morrison's novel, rememory "is something which possesses (or haunts) one, rather than something which one possesses" (p. 67). In the passage above, the past is always there, "waiting for you," waiting to bring some memory of slavery to life as a thought-picture, a rememory. So Sethe and Paul D spend much of the novel trying *not* to remember, trying to start each day with the "serious work of beating back the past" (p. 86). Because of the silences of history, because of the gaps in written slave narratives, because of the traumatic memories the survivors bear, Morrison's novel demonstrates that psychoanalytic theory is as important as historical context when approaching this subject matter.

Morrison's ability to translate the history of slavery and the Margaret Garner story into the evocative narrative strategies, prose style, and characters of *Beloved* is a strategic intervention into the problem of speaking the unspeakable. Most of all, as Morrison explains in her interview with Bonnie Angelo, she wanted to tell a personal and intimate story about slaves under slavery: "The book was not about the institution – Slavery with a capital S. It was about these anonymous people called slaves" (1989c, p. 257). This is one of the great achievements of Morrison's novel: she takes inspiration from actual historical events and people, but she breathes life into them and draws her readers into their intimate agonies, desires, humiliations, and hopes. Even the house where Sethe and Denver live takes on a life of its own. The first sentences of the novel read, "124 was spiteful. Full of a baby's venom" (p. 3). In her groundbreaking essay "Unspeakable Things Unspoken," Morrison has commented that these lines are deliberately unsettling:

> The reader is snatched, yanked, thrown into an environment completely foreign, and I want it as the first stroke of the shared experience that might be possible between the reader and the novel's population. Snatched just as the slaves were from one place to another, from any place to another, without preparation and without defense. (1989b, p. 32)

Readers enter the novel without defense, as Morrison says, snatched up in circumstances beyond their knowledge, struggle to gain their footing, and, as a result of these challenges, begin to glimpse what it might mean for Sethe, Paul D, Baby Suggs, Stamp Paid, and so many other former slaves, to struggle toward freedom and to claim possession of themselves. In the pages of *Beloved*, readers encounter a story in which the world of mid-nineteenth-century America becomes a powerful and vivid "rememory" resurrecting the lives of black women, men, children, and families left forgotten for far too long.

QUESTIONS FOR FURTHER ANALYSIS

1. Morrison takes a few of her character names directly from the historical incident that inspired *Beloved*; other names she comes up with on her own. Names suggest not only familial ties in Morrison's novel, but they are also symbolically significant. As Avery F. Gordon suggests, Morrison often creates names that "sign a life, a set of memories, a history" (p. 188). Make a chart of names and name changes for key characters in the novel; also list the animals or objects that are given names in the novel. Using this information, consider how Morrison uses names to convey larger themes and conflicts in *Beloved*.

2. In her essay "The Site of Memory," Morrison presents a paradox in describing how she moves beyond facts and claims the freedom of imagination and invention in order to tell the truth about black lives under slavery. She explains that "the crucial distinction for me is not the difference between fact and fiction, but the distinction between fact and truth. Because facts can exist without human intelligence, but truth cannot" (1987a, p. 113). How might this distinction apply to *Beloved*? What truths of slavery emerge from Morrison's decision to deviate from some of the facts of the Margaret Garner case? How might memory and imagination alleviate the silences of official histories?

CHAPTER 2

RE-MEMBERING MOTHERS AND DAUGHTERS

Motherlines lie at the heart of *Beloved*, as Mae G. Henderson has suggested. When readers begin the novel, they enter a mother–daughter household located at 124 Bluestone Road that is fraught with the complex legacies slavery inflicted on mother-hood and mothering for black women. Sethe and Denver live in the house together, a mother and daughter who have remained vitally connected despite slavery and its aftermath. But they live in isolation: Sethe's sons/Denver's brothers, Howard and Buglar, have run away from home approximately 9 years earlier, and since the death of Baby Suggs, Sethe's mother-in-law and Denver's grandmother, 8 years earlier, few visitors have come to 124. Sethe's and Denver's relationship embodies both the strengths of and the costs to black motherhood deriving from slavery.

Under slavery, in the plantation hierarchy, black women who became pregnant were sometimes given lighter chores or assigned house duties rather than field work, since they were seen as a means of reproducing labor and wealth for their white masters. But pregnancy was often forced upon black women under slavery as they were subject to rape, sexual exploitation, and studding by white masters and their sons, by white overseers and other authorities. On the other hand, pregnancy might be welcomed by black women who were allowed to couple with their husbands or partners. But becoming a mother physiologically through pregnancy carried no guarantee that a black woman might be allowed to engage in mothering. There were numerous ways in which the slave system could separate mother and child, thereby disrupting the mothering relationship, such as by assigning the mother to field work once she delivered or by selling her children to another owner. Furthermore, black women who had given birth were often assigned the role of wet nurse to the white children of the master, and so their mother's milk might not be available for their own biological children.

Beloved dramatically registers the violence done to motherhood and mothering by the slave system. As Barbara Schapiro observes, Morrison's novel is concerned with the ways that a "racist, slave society" places constraints upon African American identity and selfhood; *Beloved*, in particular, shows how "the mother, the child's first vital other, is made unreliable or unavailable by a slave system which either separates her from her child or so enervates and depletes her that she has no self from which to confer recognition" (p. 194). In Barbara Hill Rigney's interpretation of the novel, "the disintegration of family, the denial of a mother's right to love her daughter . . . is perhaps the greatest horror of the black experience under slavery" (p. 68). This chapter draws upon the work of black feminist theory to analyze mothers and daughters in Morrison's novel, paying close attention especially to Baby Suggs, Sethe, and Denver, to show the violence done to mothering by slavery and to identify the ways to resist and counteract that violence outlined by the novel.

Morrison's novel demonstrates how tenuous the connections between black mothers and their children were under slavery. Baby Suggs, one of the central mother figures in the novel, has birthed eight children, but she is allowed to remain in contact with only one of them – Halle, who as an adult works to buy his mother's freedom, but in the end does not escape slavery himself. That her eight children have had six different fathers also is worth noting, since it testifies to the exploitation and commodification of black women's bodies under slavery. Two of Baby's girls are sold without her knowledge before she can even say goodbye to them; her third child, the result of a bargain she has made to sleep with the "straw boss" in return for not selling the baby boy, is traded just a year later for a load of lumber; her fourth child is probably the result of rape – so traumatic is this experience of sexual exploitation and disrupted mothering that Baby thinks to herself, "That child she could not love and the rest she would not" (p. 28). Even worse, Baby Suggs realizes that not only are her children lost to her, but her memories of them are fading as well: "My firstborn," Baby laments to Sethe, "All I can remember of her is how she loved the burned bottom of bread. Can you beat that? Eight children and that's all I remember" (p. 6).

Baby's experience of child-loss as a mother has a corollary in Sethe's experience of mother-loss as a daughter. Just as Baby has only fading memories of her children, Sethe has only vague memories of her own mother. Sethe's mother is required to return to fieldwork just a few weeks after giving birth, so Sethe is nursed and cared for by others. Sethe has little contact with her mother, as she explains to Beloved: "By the time I woke up in the morning, she was in line. If the moon was bright they worked by its light. Sunday she slept like a stick. . . . She didn't even sleep in the same cabin most nights I remember. Too far from the line-up, I guess" (p. 72). The one vivid memory Sethe has of her mother is when her mother takes her apart from the others to show her the mark she has on her ribs – "a circle and a cross burnt right in the skin" – and tells her, "I am the only one got this mark now. The rest dead. If something happens to me and you can't tell me by my face, you can know me by this mark" (p. 72). What must it be like for a daughter to be unable to recognize her own mother by her face, to be able to identify her only by scarred flesh in the form of a brand? Sethe's mother's words dramatize the cruel disconnections slavery wrought between mothers and daughters. Her words also speak to the harrowing circumstances of slaves, who might be beaten beyond recognition or sent to a cruel death on the whim of white masters and overseers. In fact, Sethe's mother anticipates the circumstances of her own death: she is among a group of slaves hanged together, for what reason readers are never told, whose bodies are left in the tree until they have passed any point of recognizability. When the young Sethe tries to look for her mother, specifically her mother's mark, among the pile of bodies, she is pulled away before she realizes there is no way to identify her and claim her.

Perhaps Sethe would remember very little of her ma'am were it not for Nan, a slave woman whose duties include taking care of Sethe and other young slave children. One day Nan takes Sethe to the side and tells her how she got her name. As Nan reveals, she and Sethe's mother traveled on the same ship from Africa to America; both were raped repeatedly by crew members on the journey. Nan tells Sethe that her mother killed the babies that resulted from being raped:

> She threw them all away but you. The one from the crew she threw away on the island. The others from more whites she also threw away. Without names, she threw them. You she gave the name of the black man. She put her arms around him. The others she did not put her arms around. Never. Never. Telling you. I am telling you, small girl Sethe. (p. 74)

Even with its shocking revelation about the sexual violence done to black women under slavery, Nan's message is surely meant to comfort Sethe after her mother's death by letting her know how special she was to her mother, special enough to name her after the man (presumably "Seth') whom she put her arms around. But it is only because of Beloved's questions about her ma'am that Sethe even recalls this memory of her absent mother's love. Immediately after this memory breaks into consciousness, Sethe experiences a "mighty wish for Baby Suggs" that "broke over her like surf" (p. 74), for Baby has helped to fill Sethe's need to be mothered, and Sethe has helped to fill the space where Baby's own children should be. The longings of black mothers and daughters are central to Morrison's novel.

Black feminist theorist Patricia Hill Collins has synthesized a critical vocabulary to describe the variety of mothering relationships found in African American women's culture, and these terms provide valuable insights into the emphasis on mothering in Morrison's novel. Hill Collins describes the role of mothering in the black community as being distributed among "blood-mothers," "extended kin networks," "fictive kin," and "other-mothers" (pp. 178–9). By extending the act of mothering to female relatives, to friends close enough to be considered family ('fictive kin'), and to women who look out for anyone in the community who needs looking after ('othermothers'), African Americans heal some of the damage done to mothering by slavery and racism. Moreover, as Stanlie M. James points out, othermothers are "critical to the survival of Black communities," especially when they become "community othermothers," who address collective concerns in order to maintain or strengthen "a sense of the community's tradition and culture" (pp. 51, 47).

Morrison's novel shares a commitment to extending the practice of mothering beyond biological ties in order to nurture individuals in need and to draw the community together. The character of Baby Suggs is exemplary in this regard. Even though slavery has forced her to bear children while at the same time denying her the opportunity to mother them, Baby Suggs does not relinquish her mothering abilities altogether. She generously conveys her mother wisdom and caring to extended kin and to people who have no direct kinship relation to her. It is Baby who tenderly bathes Sethe and looks after her whipped and bloody back, her swollen and injured feet, when Sethe arrives in Ohio after escaping Sweet Home; it is Baby who puts the newborn Denver to Sethe's breast and encourages her to nurse. It is Baby who remains a constant presence in Sethe's and Denver's lives, even after the Misery and Sethe's jail time. Baby Suggs, denied the right to mother her own biological children, pours her heart into caring for Sethe as though she were her own daughter, and provides Denver with a constant source of grandmotherly and motherly love and wisdom, especially when Sethe is not available physically or psychologically.

Baby Suggs also functions as a community othermother when she puts her heart to work and becomes "an unchurched preacher," who calls ex-slaves together in the Clearing and urges them to love themselves (p. 102). In Trudier Harris's words, "As a holy woman . . . Baby Suggs uses her heart to become the heart of the community" (1991, p. 174). In the Clearing, Baby starts by calling children to come forward, then mothers, and then men: insisting on this order, she restores crucial bonds that slavery severed, beginning with mothers and their children, for this reunification is primary and makes it possible to reunite black families and to heal the black community. Then Baby preaches her own gospel to the black community in the Clearing, a gospel that encourages the reclaiming of bodies, the love of oneself:

'Here," she said, "in this here place, we flesh; flesh that weeps, laughs; flesh that dances on bare feet in grass. Love it. Love it hard. Yonder they do not love your flesh. They despise it. They don't love your eyes; they'd just as soon pick em out. No more do they love the skin on your back. Yonder they flay it. And O my people they do not love your hands. Those they only use, tie, bind, chop off and leave empty. Love your hands! Love them. Raise them up and kiss them. Touch others with them, pat them together, stroke them on your face 'cause they don't love that either. *You* got to love it, *you!*" (pp. 103–4)

She continues her preaching, urging her audience in turn to love their mouths, their feet, their necks, all their inside parts, their sexual organs, and especially their heart: "More than your life-holding womb and your life-giving private parts, hear me now, love your heart. For this is the prize" (p. 104). Baby's sermon skillfully deconstructs the dehumanizing and soul-numbing ideology of slavery and passionately inserts in its place a celebration of flesh, black selfhood, love, and spirituality. As Linda Krumholz describes her, "Baby Suggs is the moral and spiritual backbone of *Beloved*" (p. 112).

Because of her generous heart and her devotion to the black community, Baby Suggs is broken when the community fails to warn her on the day that schoolteacher and his posse come to claim ownership of Sethe and her children. How could someone so devoted to community othermothering fail to be cared for in return? Morrison's novels are careful not to romanticize black community, and *Beloved* is no exception. The community that Baby Suggs has spent so much time nurturing and healing is susceptible to jealousy – jealousy caused by Sethe, who has managed to escape slavery along with all her children, jealousy over the elaborate feast that Baby and Stamp Paid have hosted to celebrate the escape – and may still be traumatized in the aftermath of slavery: in other words, not healed enough to the point to be able to care unconditionally for a fellow ex-slave. Whatever the reason, the community fails Baby Suggs, fails Sethe and her children, fails to be a protective mothering presence on the day that schoolteacher comes to 124 Bluestone Road.

As Sethe thinks back to 1855 from the day she returns to the Clearing in 1873 to remember Baby Suggs, she understands something important: "Freeing yourself was one thing; claiming ownership of that freed self was another" (pp. 111–12). One of the aspects of freedom that matters most to Sethe throughout the novel is the freedom to be a mother, to love her children without fear or restraint. So crucial is mothering to Sethe's sense of her own self-identity and self-worth that milk is the key image associated with her. The significance of mother's milk flows throughout the novel, as Sethe is proud of the fact that she had "milk enough for all" when she arrives with newborn Denver at 124 Bluestone Road in 1855 to find her three other children safe with Baby Suggs (p. 233), and she continues to use those same terms in affirmative moments elsewhere in the novel (see, for example, p. 118).

Sethe's fierce attachment to motherhood and mothering is heroic, on the one hand, and potentially dangerous, on the other. Jean Wyatt describes the heroic aspect of the novel effectively: "Sethe's self-definition as maternal body enables Morrison to construct a new narrative form – a specifically female quest powered by the desire to get one's milk to one's baby – that features childbirth as high adventure" (p. 475). Indeed, Sethe is driven by the impulse to be a mother to her children in a way that her own ma'am never could: Sethe, who had "no nursing milk to call my own," because her mother had to return to fieldwork and because Nan had to nurse the white babies before she could turn to Sethe, vows that "Nobody will ever get my milk no more except my own children" (p. 236).

But it is hard for other characters in the novel to understand fully Sethe's extravagant claims to milk and mothering. Even someone as sympathetically inclined as Paul D does not quite grasp Sethe's emphasis on her milk. In the opening scene of the novel, as Paul D and Sethe are getting reacquainted, she tells him about the incident when schoolteacher's nephews held her down, stole her milk, and then whipped her after learning that she told Mrs. Garner about what they did. What is striking is that Sethe and Paul D have quite different views about what is most violent in the incident:

"They used cowhide on you?"
"And they took my milk."
"They beat you and you was pregnant?"
"And they took my milk!" (p. 20)

In their exchange, Paul D emphasizes the cruelty of whipping, especially of whipping a pregnant woman, while Sethe sees the stealing of her milk, symbolizing a threat to her capacity to mother her children, as the real crime. The fact that their views are so divergent is underscored in the passage by Sethe's repetition of the same phrase to try to make her point clear (with an exclamation point added to the second iteration). Paul D, who has learned to love small so that he will not be disappointed, sees that Sethe has not learned, and is not interested in learning, his survival strategy of carefully controlled, restricted loving. In his way of looking at things, Sethe is flirting with disaster: "Risky, thought Paul D, very risky. For a used-to-be-slave woman to love anything that much was dangerous, especially if it was her children she had settled on to love" (p. 54).

At some level, Sethe understands the potential dangers of fiercely attached mothering; she thinks to herself, "Unless carefree, motherlove was a killer" (p. 155). Of course, for Sethe, these words about motherlove are literally true. When Paul D confronts her with the newspaper article Stamp Paid has given him, Sethe first tries to explain the strength of her love for her children as she experienced it once she escaped from Sweet Home: "when I stretched out my arms all my children could get in between. I was *that* wide. Look like I loved em more after I got here. Or maybe I couldn't love em proper in Kentucky because they wasn't mine to love" (p. 190). Sethe here speaks of one of the greatest tolls slavery exacted on black women – the unfathomable pain of having children they could never count on calling their own. Slavery as a system not only separated mother and child routinely and cruelly; it also, as Morrison's novel points out, made mothers afraid to love their children completely. It is only once she gets to Ohio that Sethe realizes that her children are hers, that her motherlove can run free. When schoolteacher appears with his posse to claim ownership of Sethe and her children, Sethe sees herself as acting in the only way she can to keep them safe from his grasp, safe from slavery: she tries to kill her children because she loves them so much.

The paradox of this statement emerges because, in effect, Sethe is caught between two ways of thinking about the world when schoolteacher catches up with her. On the one hand, she has experienced 28 days of freedom, of being able to love her children from the bottom of her heart, 28 days that have taught her the depth and beauty of that love so that she cannot go back to what it was like before. On the other hand, schoolteacher's presence suggests the inescapability of the slave system in 1855, especially once the Fugitive Slave Law of 1850 extended the reach of slavery into free states like Ohio; slavery as a system that dealt in human beings as property insists that Sethe has no rights as a mother, no claim to motherlove, because she is less than human. When Sethe slits the throat of her dearly beloved baby girl, she demonstrates that both interpretations are true: she indeed acts out of the fullness of her love for her children, and she does so in a dramatic, bloody act that calls attention to the violence of slavery. Because of these overlapping meanings, all of the onlookers are horrified – schoolteacher and Baby Suggs, Stamp Paid and the white posse. In effect, what Sethe does is so unfathomable that she is displaced from both systems: schoolteacher decides something is so wrong with Sethe that she is not fit to be a slave any longer, and he abandons any attempt to claim his so-called property, and the black community begins to shun Sethe and 124 Bluestone Road.

Beloved, as the title of the novel itself suggests, is about the expression and consequences of loving one's children within and despite the slave system. *Beloved* asks readers to consider the difficult ethical question of how to judge Sethe's act of love, which is also, at the same time, an act of murder. Because this question is so complicated, the novel offers several points of view on the ethical implications of Sethe's actions. Sethe herself emphasizes the need to keep her children safe from slavery: she explains to Paul D, "I stopped him" (referring to schoolteacher) – "I took and put my babies where they'd be safe." But Paul D bluntly replies, "Your love is too thick" (p. 193). "Love is or it ain't. Thin love ain't love at all," Sethe counters. Paul D's response – "What you did was wrong, Sethe" – shows that he cannot understand at all how love could lead to killing (p. 194).

Certainly, Sethe's killing of Beloved has severe consequences for other characters in the novel. Baby Suggs loses the Call and never again returns to the Clearing to preach her gospel of self-love, then takes to bed and ponders individual colors until she is released into death. Denver is also adversely affected by Sethe's act of rough motherlove. Interested in learning to read and write, Denver in her girlhood begins going to school at Miss Lady Jones's house, where, one day, little Nelson Lord asks Denver a question about Sethe that makes Denver lose all sense of hearing for a couple of years rather than listen to her mother's response to the question. Even after her hearing is restored, Denver is cut off from the world around her; after she stops going to school, she never again leaves the house by herself. Instead she spends her days worrying that some stranger might enter the yard of 124 again and make it possible for Sethe to kill *her* this time, so she stays home, constantly watching the yard and trying to protect herself and her mother. Denver also has terrible recurring dreams – "She cut my head off every night" (p. 243); and she warns Beloved, "Don't love her too much. Don't. Maybe it's still in her the thing that makes it all right to kill her children" (p. 243). Ironically, tragically, Sethe's claims to love her children freely result in Denver's deeply rooted fear of loving her mother.

From Beloved's point of view, as Sethe's returned-from-the-grave daughter (see the next chapter for a full analysis of her character), Sethe's motherlove is both "too thick" and too "thin." Her anger and sadness haunt 124 Bluestone Road, constantly reminding Sethe of her death and isolating Sethe as the novel opens. When Beloved appears as a young woman, she at first dotes on Sethe, feasting her eyes on her, dwelling on every word, drawing out stories from Sethe that she has not remembered in years. But Sethe's daily routine – her relationship with Paul D, going to work, tending to chores and other people – naturally involves time away from Beloved that becomes an ungovernable loss for her. Beloved chokes Sethe, eventually demands all her attention, and is never satisfied (or satisfiable). While Sethe initially is overjoyed to recognize Beloved as her daughter because she thinks all is forgiven, nothing could be further from the truth. Beloved demands everything from Sethe, and Sethe, in a vain attempt to atone for the murder, sacrifices everything for Beloved.

The dangerous imbalance in their relationship that emerges as the novel progresses has fueled critical debate about what goes wrong in the reunification of mother and daughter. Is Sethe's love indeed "too thick," as Paul D suggests? Some scholars agree with his pronouncement, while others take a more sympathetic or complex view of Sethe's motherlove. One scholar who takes the former approach is Stephanie A. Demetrakopoulos, who has provocatively argued that *Beloved* demonstrates "the devouring nature of maternal bonds" (p. 52). For Demetrakopoulos, Sethe's decision to kill Beloved and to try to kill her other children when confronted by schoolteacher is a gruesome way of protecting them: she "devour[s] them back into the security of womb/tomb death" (p. 53). The devouring nature of maternal bonding harms Sethe as well: Demetrakopoulos points out that Sethe immerses herself to such an extreme degree in her role as a mother that she loses any sense of her own individuality, and only with the help of a community of mothers, who know the costs and guilt that mothering can inflict, can Sethe break free. In Demetrakopoulos's interpretation, the novel "examines the death of the maternal in a woman so that her Self might live" (p. 58).

While Demetrakopoulos's feminist reading of the novel emphasizes mothering as a potentially all-consuming, and hence dangerous, force in a woman's life and sees the novel as affirming the importance of female/feminist selfhood, other scholars connect the dangers of mothering to historical forces, especially slavery. Jean Wyatt, in contrast to Demetrakopoulos, sees slavery rather than excessive mothering as the most important factor behind Sethe's killing of Beloved:

Sethe extends her rights over her own body – the right to use any means, including death, to protect herself from a return to slavery – to the "parts of her" that are her children, folding them back into the maternal body in order to enter death as a single unit (though she succeeded in killing only one of her daughters). The novel withholds judgment on Sethe's act and persuades the reader to do the same, presenting the infanticide as the ultimate contradiction of mothering under slavery. (p. 476)

While Wyatt is attentive to the violence of slavery that influences Sethe's act, she also goes on in her reading of the novel to use psychoanalytic theory to identify deficits in Sethe's subjectivity as a mother.

One scholar who unequivocally endorses Sethe's mothering is Andrea O'Reilly, who argues that her capacity for "thick love" is what makes Sethe heroic:

Sethe comes to love her self in loving her children and the strong selfhood she eventually creates for herself is formed from her maternal heroism. Sethe must learn to love herself as she loves her children, and love her children as they need to be loved. Both acts are possible because Sethe has been blessed with a generous "thick love". (p. 138)

One might argue, however, that it is not Sethe's mothering capacity that restores her to herself at the end of the novel, but her capacity to be nurtured (or mothered) in the form of Denver's heroic decision to go out in the world and try to save Sethe from Beloved, as well as Paul D's return to 124 Bluestone Road to rub Sethe's feet and to tell her, "You your best thing, Sethe. You are" (p. 322). Perhaps the heroism of Sethe's thick love is best seen by the fact that it inspires reciprocal loving acts from others.

Carole Boyce Davies points out that "the attempt to construct Sethe as resisting mother is highly charged but also problematic" (p. 53), for in her view, Sethe is caught between contradictory ideologies. Sethe's motherlove, as Davies describes it, is definitely "too-thick", as Paul D says, because it too fully accepts the given paradigm of motherhood as exclusive responsibility of the biological mother. . . . A slave mother is not supposed to demonstrate deep love for her children. Sethe defies that. Yet her heroic response to enslavement paradoxically becomes the kind of motherlove which society enforces for women. Sethe shuttles back and forth between enslavements, exchanging one for the other, unable to be freed from both at once. (p. 54)

Davies stresses the importance of recognizing the complexities of the novel in presenting Sethe's actions and in shaping readers' reactions to them.

As Davies's comments suggest, the question of Sethe's motherlove being too thick or thin leads to significant ethical interpretations of the novel. Postcolonial theorist Homi Bhabha writes sympathetically of the central ethical quandary in the novel, calling attention to Sethe's marginal and wounded status: "As we reconstruct the narrative of child murder through Sethe, the slave mother, who is herself the victim of social death, the very historical basis of our ethical judgement undergoes a radical revision" (p. 16). In a 1989 interview with Bill Moyers, Morrison herself has commented on the ethical dilemma that confronts Sethe in language that simultaneously affirms and disavows the killing of her baby. Referring to Margaret Garner's story, Morrison initially describes the killing as a heroic act of love: "Shall I permit my children, who are my best thing, to live like I have lived, when I know that's terrible? So she decided to kill them and kill herself. That was noble. She was saying, "I'm a human being. These are my children"." But Morrison goes on, just a few moments later, to acknowledge the act as a terrible choice, quoting a line from an acquaintance: "'It was the right thing to do, but she had no right to do it'" (1989d, p. 272).

Morrison's sense of the complex ethical dilemma facing Sethe (and readers) complements Ashraf Rushdy's reading of the novel's ability to "accuse and embrace" Sethe at the same time. Like Bhabha, Rushdy insists on linking history to ethics in the novel: "Morrison insists on the impossibility of judging an action without reference to the terms of its enactment – the wrongness of assuming a transhistorical ethic outside a particular historical moment" (p. 577). One way that Morrison's novel creates a historical context for pondering Sethe's killing of Beloved, Rushdy observes, is by portraying other slave mothers in the novel (Sethe's ma'am and Ella, for instance) who have also been provoked to infanticide because of the terrors of slavery. But Rushdy also sees the two daughters in *Beloved* as representing two contrasting ways of judging Sethe's actions. For Rushdy, Beloved "is the daughter representing a severe critique," and Denver is "the daughter of hope'; Beloved functions as "the incarnated memory of Sethe's guilt" and is the "symbol of an unrelenting criticism of the dehumanizing function of the institution of slavery," while Denver is the daughter who symbolizes the need to remember the past in order to bring about "an affirmative return to life" (p. 578).

Denver has a special role to play in understanding the ethical dilemmas of the novel, for as Rushdy points out, Denver occupies "the space for hearing the tale of infanticide with a degree of understanding – both as sister of the murdered baby and as the living daughter of the loving mother" (p. 586). Because Denver is fearful of her mother, still feels the loss of her Grandma Baby, and has been isolated from the community for so many years, she eagerly accepts Beloved into the household. Longing for companionship, Denver showers Beloved with attention and care, and she recognizes Beloved as her sister almost immediately (much sooner, in fact, than Sethe recognizes Beloved as her daughter). Denver's loneliness has been so painful that her need for Beloved's presence quickly takes precedence over her loyalty to her mother. After the incident in the Clearing when Beloved begins to choke Sethe, Denver realizes she wants Beloved to be "*hers*" no matter what: "Denver was alarmed by the harm she thought Beloved planned for Sethe, but felt helpless to thwart it, so unrestricted was her need to love another. The display she witnessed at the Clearing shamed her because the choice between Sethe and Beloved was without conflict" (p. 123).

For much of the novel, there is no conflict over which side Denver will take: she sides with Beloved. But readers have to ask whether Denver's unquestioning loyalty to Beloved is linked to her sense that Beloved has been horribly wronged by Sethe or whether it occurs because Denver has felt so unloved by or fearful of Sethe that she cannot sympathize with her mother. Eventually, however, Denver does indeed become alarmed by Beloved's treatment of Sethe, and she decides to get help. Two mothering women from her past enable Denver to leave home and go into the outside world: Baby Suggs and Lady Jones. Denver remembers that, while Grandma Baby was alive, she taught Denver important lessons about loving her body and not feeling guilty about pleasure, about how she didn't need to fear the baby ghost of 124, about how her father was an "Angel man" and about how "charmed" Denver herself is (pp. 246–7). Even after death, Baby Suggs continues as a motherly presence in Denver's life. When Denver decides to leave the house on her own for the first time in years, to get help for Sethe, it is her grandma's laugh and words she hears, coming to her from the beyond, urging her forward:

> You mean I never told you nothing about Carolina? About your daddy? You don't remember nothing about how come I walk the way I do and about your mother's feet, not to speak of her back? I never told you all that? Is that why you can't walk down the steps? My Jesus my. (pp. 287–8)

By putting Denver's fears in the context of what her family has endured, Baby Suggs convinces Denver to conquer her fears and to step off the porch. Baby Suggs's grandmotherly nudging propels Denver onto the porch of another house where another other-mother is waiting for her: Mrs. Lady Jones. Lady Jones not only welcomes Denver into her house, she feeds her literally and emotionally. All Denver has to do is ask for help and explain why ('My ma'am, she doesn't feel good'), and Lady Jones responds immediately with empathy and understanding—' "Oh, baby," said Mrs. Jones. 'Oh baby'" (p. 292) – and then with food to take home and the promise of more to come. Most important, the encounter with

Lady Jones changes Denver inside: "She did not know it then, but it was the word "baby," said softly and with such kindness, that inaugurated her life in the world as a woman" (p. 292).

Stepping into the outside world, on her own, Denver grows up quickly and is able to see that the relationship between Sethe and Beloved has become dangerously inverted: "Beloved bending over Sethe looked the mother, Sethe the teething child. . . . The bigger Beloved got, the smaller Sethe became" (p. 294). Denver begins to understand that the two are trapped in a vicious circle: "Sethe was trying to make up for the handsaw; Beloved was making her pay for it. But there would never be an end to that, and seeing her mother diminished shamed and infuriated her" (p. 295). Even though Denver is 18 years old when the novel opens, she has been so cut off from the rest of the world, so reliant on her mother alone, that she seems years younger than her age for most of the narrative. But the Denver who recognizes that something terribly wrong is happening between her mother and Beloved is a mature young woman, who is beginning to understand the complexities behind the terrible choice her mother made on the day of the Misery.

This grown-up Denver, who is able to step off the porch at 124 into the outside world, sets in motion a chain of events that culminates in a climactic scene of community othermothering. In order to secure a job with the Bodwins, Denver has to reveal to Janey that Beloved, the murdered daughter, has returned and is tormenting Sethe. As Janey spreads the word, the women of the community weigh the news, and while some are quick to say "Guess she had it coming," Ella immediately counters with "What's fair ain't necessarily right" (p. 301). Ella decides that something must be done for Sethe, before the "devil-child" kills the mother (p. 308), and she organizes a group of women to go to 124 to exorcise the demon. They come to pray and sing exactly at the right moment: their presence not only makes Beloved disappear, they also prevent Sethe from repeating another violent act based on desperate motherlove when she sees Mr. Edward Bodwin's hat and mistakes it for schoolteacher's.

The treatment of mothers and daughters in *Beloved* is richly complex. On one level, Morrison's novel undoes some of the damage inflicted by slavery by depicting mothers and daughters in the novel who long for each other even when they might not remain physically present to each other. Morrison's novel dynamically re-members and reconnects black mothers and daughters. On another level, however, the novel cautions against the desire for mothers to try to assuage all the pain inflicted by slavery and racism. No one mother can shoulder such a burden. In the end, Morrison's novel dramatically underscores the need for black women to support each other, to serve as surrogate mothers and othermothers, for only by extending mothering beyond kin and by practicing collective acts of mothering can the black community be sustained.

QUESTIONS FOR FURTHER ANALYSIS

1. This chapter has focused on motherhood as a significant physiological, psychological, and social function for black women in *Beloved*. Is mothering a role and function reserved only for black women in the novel, or can black men be motherly too? Why might it be useful to extend the role of mothering beyond biology or reproductive capability to include men as well?

2. While Sethe and Beloved's relationship has received the greatest attention in reviews and scholarly articles on Morrison's novel, one might argue that Denver's presence in the narrative is subtle at times, yet crucial. Think closely about Denver's education and development in the novel. How does Beloved change her? What kind of woman do you suppose Denver becomes after the novel closes? How does Denver's development illuminate key themes of the novel?

CHAPTER 3

THE UNCANNY PRESENCE OF BELOVED

How is it possible to uncover and narrate a history that no one wants to face? While Toni Morrison's Beloved is based on a historical child named Mary Garner (as explained in Chapter 1), it is also clear that the character signifies much more than this particular child and incident. Beloved comes to embody not only Sethe's dead daughter, but also represents the traumatic wounds of slavery: wounds so gaping that no one wants to see them, know them, or re-memory them, because they can never be sutured or healed completely. Because of Morrison's powerful creation of Beloved as a character, she is an enigma who has invited a wide range of scholarly commentary. This chapter focuses first on key aspects of Morrison's depiction of Beloved, then turns to various interpretations of what she represents in the novel.

Beloved appears in the novel first as a spirit who disrupts everyday life at 124 Bluestone Road. When Paul D enters the house in 1873, he has to step through "a pool of red and undulating light" that he first suspects might be evil, but Sethe informs him, "It's not evil, just sad," and tells him the spirit belongs to her dead daughter (p. 10). Then the quaking begins and the house literally rocks on its foundations, as it has been doing for years, having driven away Sethe's sons, Howard and Buglar, and now apparently trying to drive away Paul D, who decides to stand his ground. When readers first encounter Beloved, she is a spirit who haunts the house, who haunts the mother who killed her. *Beloved* begins as a story about a ghost, but soon becomes much more.

Paul D silences the ghost, but once it appears that he, Sethe, and Denver might be able to establish their own family group, a young black woman in need of help appears outside 124 and is taken in by Sethe. Oddly enough, she gives her name as Beloved – the same name that appears on the tombstone for Sethe's dead daughter. Even though she has the shape of a 19 or 20-year-old woman, there are some puzzling features about Beloved: she has labored breath, as though she is unused to breathing on her own; her skin is "unlined," apparently unmarked like a newborn baby's; she cannot at first hold her head up; she can barely walk, which Sethe and Paul D take as a sign of illness; she sleeps a lot; she has an unquenchable thirst; her language is stilted, and she cannot read, which Paul D takes as a sign of the illiteracy enforced by most slaveowners; she does not know how to tie her own shoes. While some of these signs can be read in other ways, together they point to Beloved's identity as Sethe's daughter, who returns at the age she would have been had she lived, but in essence is still the young "crawling-already?" baby girl (p. 110) that Sethe killed. Somehow, the ghost has become enfleshed, has taken on bodily form, to appear and reclaim Sethe's attention.

Further evidence accumulates identifying Beloved as Sethe's resurrected baby girl. Catching sight of the young woman, Sethe has an uncontrollable urge to empty her bladder, which brings to mind the day she went into labor with Denver while she was trying to flee slavery: "But there was no stopping water breaking from a breaking womb and there was no stopping now" (p. 61). Here Boy, the dog who has been terrified by the ghost's whims in the past, disappears the day Beloved arrives and does not return until she is gone at the end of the novel. Denver seems almost immediately to recognize the young woman as her sister, especially since the young woman asks questions of Sethe (about her earrings, for example) and seems to know songs and other things that only Sethe's daughter could know. And then there are the physical marks: the scar on her neck, caused by the handsaw that Sethe used to slit her throat open, that Denver sees only at night when Beloved changes to night clothes, as well as the three vertical lines on Beloved's forehead, caused by Sethe's fingernails in the woodshed as she struggled to hold her daughter's severed head on her body as the blood seeped out.

Beloved also has supernatural abilities. She seems to know what Paul D is thinking when he vows to himself to do some investigating about her in town; at the very moment he is having this private thought, she chokes on her food, falls off her chair, and has to be resuscitated (p. 79). In the Clearing, where Sethe goes one day to sit and remember Baby Suggs, Sethe feels a spirit first rubbing her shoulders, then choking her; Denver not only runs to help Sethe, she quickly realizes that Beloved has been doing the choking from afar (p. 119). Denver is also privy to Beloved's ability to disappear, then reappear, inexplicably, as she does one day right before Denver's eyes when they are in the cold house fetching a jug of cider (pp. 144–5). Paul D too experiences the extraordinary powers of Beloved, when she moves him away from Sethe's bed, into the rocking chair, then the keeping room, then the cold house – out of the house toward her, as she commands him to "touch me on the inside part and call me my name" (p. 137).

Further heightening the enigmatic presence of Beloved – her inexplicable return from the dead to be present in the flesh in 1873 – is the fact that in other respects Morrison's novel is quite realistic, especially in its unflinching treatment of slavery. Some scholars and reviewers have employed the term "magical realism" for Morrison's novels to describe the extraordinary elements mixed together with the cultural and social realism found within them. While this term might be one way to understand *Beloved*, Morrison in fact has expressed dissatisfaction with this approach to her novels. In an interview with Christina Davis, for instance, Morrison comments that the term "magical realism" "was a way of *not* talking about the politics. It was a way of *not* talking about what was in the books," and she goes on to emphasize that, in her perspective, "the word "magical" . . . *dilutes* the realism" (1986, p. 226). When reading *Beloved*, then, it is important not to situate the "magical" in a way that would dilute the realism; rather, it is crucial to find a way to interpret the supernatural presence and capabilities of Beloved as necessarily interconnected to the realities of black lives experiencing slavery and struggling toward freedom in mid-nineteenth-century America. Freud's theory of the uncanny can be helpful in this regard, for Freud insists that the uncanny emerges when "the distinction between imagination and reality is effaced, as when something that we have hitherto regarded as imaginary appears before us in reality, or when a symbol takes over the full functions of the thing it symbolizes" (p. 145). For Freud, the uncanny is not the opposite of something that is familiar or ordinary; rather, "the *unheimlich* is what was once *heimisch*, familiar; the prefix *un* [un-] is the token of repression" (p. 146). Throughout Morrison's novel, Beloved hovers in this space where the ordinary becomes extraordinary, where something that should be familiar seems strange and unfamiliar.

Martha Cutter notes that "even as the text produces evidence that supports a realistic explanation of Beloved's presence, it also continually draws us back into the realm of the marvelous" (p. 65). For Cutter, this ambiguity is crucial in order to resist closure and to keep the narrative in motion so that the story will be remembered. Indeed, the novel presents copious evidence of Beloved's surreal/magical identity as Sethe's returned-from-the-dead daughter, while it also offers evidence that situates Beloved in a realistic framework.

Let us consider realistic explanations first. When Paul D first becomes suspicious about who Beloved might be, one of the possibilities he considers is that she is a young black woman in need of protection: "It was one thing to beat up a ghost, quite another to throw a helpless coloredgirl out in territory infected by the Klan. Desperately thirsty for black blood, without which it could not live, the dragon swam the Ohio at will" (p. 79). The vulnerable position young black women found themselves in, even after the end of slavery, is further confirmed by Sethe's telling Denver that "she believed Beloved had been locked up by some whiteman for his own purposes, and never let out the door. That she must have escaped to a bridge or someplace and rinsed the rest out of her mind" (p. 140). Near the end of the novel, a similar scenario is mentioned by Stamp Paid: "Was a girl locked up in the house with a whiteman over by Deer Creek. Found him dead last summer and the girl gone. Maybe that's her. Folks say he had her in there since she was a pup" (p. 277). Ella's own experience of being locked up "in a house where she was shared by father and son, whom she called 'the lowest yet'" (p. 301) further demonstrates the traumatic experiences black women faced. Morrison's novel provides ample evidence that Beloved is in fact a homeless and friendless black woman who has escaped sexual enslavement by white male tormentors.

That explanation, however, does not account for everything that unfolds in the novel. Trying to solve the puzzle of Beloved's identity, readers may begin to grasp the fascinating and unsettling set of interpretive possibilities she represents. Indeed, in each of the novel's three main sections, Beloved accrues new meanings. In part one of the novel, she is literally a young black woman in need, but she is also a ghost who sparks memories that the occupants of 124 have forgotten or never shared before. Beloved may be effectively linked to the Freudian concept of the "return of the repressed": literally, she returns as the murdered daughter who has been forgotten by the community, but she also represents other memories that Paul D and Sethe have successfully repressed for years. Paul D, who has been able to lock away everything in what he pictures as a tobacco tin kept inside his chest where his heart used to be, begins to remember Alfred, Georgia, and a rooster named Mister (discussed in detail in the following chapter). Sethe begins to recall her ma'am and the earrings Mrs. Garner gave her, and she is able to tell these formerly untold stories to Denver and Beloved. As Deborah Horvitz notes, "Beloved generates a metamorphosis in Sethe that allows her to speak what she had thought to be the unspeakable" (p. 158). This is dramatically demonstrated when Paul D and Sethe finally share their stories about their last days at Sweet Home, and Paul D reveals that Halle saw what schoolteacher's nephews did to Sethe and that it broke him. This is also when Paul D tells Sethe for the first time about having the bit placed on him. Denver, too, has reawakened memories in Beloved's presence: she remembers going to school for a year at Lady Jones's house, until the day when Nelson Lord asked about her mother and Denver lost her hearing.

Bringing the past to life literally and psychologically culminates at the end of Part One of the novel, when finally the silence surrounding what has gone unspoken for so long is broken. Stamp Paid shows Paul D the clipping about Sethe's act of "rough motherlove'; readers for the first time are told the story of the day when schoolteacher rides to 124 to reclaim his "property" in vivid, disquieting detail; and then Paul D tries to talk with Sethe about what happened that day, only to fail to understand or sympathize with her explanation. The return of the repressed can result in eye-opening, disturbing moments of recognition, and indeed this happens in *Beloved* as Part One draws to a close and everything seems to be falling apart. Beloved's presence, and catalyzing influence, in Part One makes possible a necessary, though painful, reckoning with the past, bringing to consciousness the tragedies and brutalities of the slave system.

In Part Two, with Paul D gone from 124 and out of Sethe's life, Beloved is named and claimed as the returned-from-the-dead daughter, when Sethe finally recognizes her. How could it take so long for Sethe to recognize her own Beloved, especially when Denver has been so quick to claim her returned sister? Sethe insists that Paul D's presence confused her and made her too distracted to recognize Beloved. It is the "humming" of a song, though, that tellingly triggers the "click" of Sethe's recognition (p. 207). Throughout the novel, characters sometimes sing what they cannot bring themselves to say directly; these songs are richly suggestive in themselves, but also indicate a coded language that is sometimes necessary to begin to breach the master's rules (as in the song that Halle sings to let the Sweet Home slaves know that it is time to put their escape plans into action), or to speak of feelings and fears so deep that only sound, without words, is possible at first. So when Beloved hums the tune of a song that Sethe made up to sing to her children when they were young, Sethe senses the undertones and her memory rushes in.

The reunion of mother and daughter is rapturous at first. Sethe is thrilled not only to have her daughter returned to her, but celebrates their perfect connection, taking heart in the fact that Beloved is not angry with her and that if Beloved can forgive her, then Sethe can stop remembering the rest of the past. In Part Two of the novel, Sethe, Denver, and Beloved become a family once again. What slavery wrenched asunder, the three women re-member: they restore motherly, daughterly, and sisterly bonds. They retreat from the outside world and create their own utopian space of reconnection inside 124, finally beginning to utter what had formerly been "unspeakable thoughts, unspoken" (which Stamp Paid interestingly hears as an "undecipherable" "roaring') (p. 235). The section of the novel that runs from pages 236 to 256 consists of interior monologues from Sethe, Denver, and Beloved, which then merge together by the end, signalling how significant the reconnection of mothers and daughters is to the novel (as discussed in the previous chapter). It is important to note that these interior monologues are not spoken aloud: what Morrison has attempted to do is to indicate the flow of thoughts in a stream of consciousness, thoughts that each woman is perhaps admitting to for the first time. Sethe's monologue naturally expresses the joy of having her daughter back, but this moment of recovery also leads to a startling recognition: the possibility that Sethe's ma'am was hanged for trying to escape slavery, and if that was indeed the case, then she was fleeing without Sethe, and abandoning her daughter. Denver's thoughts reflect a similar mixture of joy and fear, and Morrison's novel suggests that psychologically good memories restore health in a way that allows for a reckoning with repressed traumatic memories. Denver celebrates being reconnected with her sister, and so protective is that feeling that she also allows herself to admit her deep fears about Sethe – that what Sethe did to Beloved, she might also be capable of doing to Denver.

Beloved's interior monologue is the most complex, however. Morrison has rendered Beloved's thoughts in densely imagistic prose, without any punctuation whatsoever, allowing spaces in the lines to signal thought-breaks – places where thoughts break down or where sentences come to an end. These innovations are necessary, for Beloved's interior monologue also reveals that she is more than Sethe's returned-from-the-dead daughter. As Morrison explained in an interview with Marsha Darling, Beloved represents two kinds of death:

She is a spirit on the one hand, literally she is what Sethe thinks she is, her child returned to her from the dead. And she must function like that in the text. She is also another kind of dead which is not spiritual but flesh, which is a survivor from the true, factual slave ship. She speaks the language, a traumatized language, of her own experience, which blends beautifully in her questions and answers, her preoccupations, with the desires of Denver and Sethe. So that when they say "What was it like over there?" they may mean – they do mean – "What was it like being dead?" She tells them what it was like being where she was on that ship as a child. Both things are possible, and there's evidence in the text so that both things could be approached, because the language of both experiences – death and the Middle Passage – is the same. Her yearning would be the same, the love and yearning for that face that was going to smile at her. (1988, p. 247)

Morrison's comments here about Beloved's link to the Middle Passage recall the dedication to the novel, which reads "Sixty Million / and more." Morrison has explained that this figure refers to an estimated number of Africans who perished in Africa being captured or who perished on the Middle Passage, who never even made it into slavery (see Clemons 1987, p. 75).

As Morrison suggests in the interview above, a close reading of Beloved's interior monologue reveals that she thinks in images drawn from the unspeakable, unspoken horrors of being captured in Africa and being confined to the hold of a ship on the Middle Passage. Beloved's first memory is of a woman she loves (her mother presumably) gathering flowers and putting them in a basket until "the clouds" get in the way and separate them (p. 248): this brief memory might be read as the moment when she and her mother are captured by slave traders in Africa, the clouds signaling gunfire. In the subsequent paragraphs of Beloved's monologue, she is on a ship, crowded and almost crushed by the other people around her: some people are dying and the others are "trying to leave our bodies behind" (pp. 248–9) because of the wretched conditions. Again, she spots the woman she longs for; this time the woman does not have the "shining in her ears" (later identified as earrings) that Beloved saw earlier, but she does have a "circle around her neck" (a metal collar or a necklace?) (p. 249). Then the woman plunges into the ocean (an act of deliberate suicide, perhaps), and so once again Beloved's monologue reflects the loss of the mother and a fear of separation. In a third broken memory, Beloved recalls being the only one left on the ship after the others have been "taken," and then she is raped: "he hurts where I sleep   he puts his finger there" (p. 251). In response to this terrible violation, she sees herself as "break[ing] into pieces" and then plunges into the water to "join" the face of the woman she longs for (p. 251). What this last memory encapsulates is not at all clear: perhaps it indicates a protective descent into madness, caused by the trauma of the rape; perhaps the rape has led to beatings or injuries that result in her death; or perhaps she leaps into water to commit suicide to escape from her tormentors.

Beloved's interior monologue is complicated in yet another way. While Sethe's and Denver's monologues immediately claim Beloved as the daughter/sister returned from the dead, Beloved does not make the link between the woman whose face she longs for and Sethe until the very end of her stream of memories:

> I am not dead   I sit   the sun closes my eye   when I open
> them I see the face I lost   Sethe's is the face that left me
> Sethe sees me see her and I see the smile (p. 252)

Does Beloved long so much for the mother she has lost that she too eagerly claims Sethe as a surrogate? Elizabeth House has argued that Beloved is not Sethe's returned daughter at all, but an actual survivor of the Middle Passage. In House's reading of the novel, Sethe and Beloved bond together out of "mistaken identity": "Beloved is haunted by the loss of her African parents and thus comes to believe that Sethe is her mother. Sethe longs for her dead daughter and is rather easily convinced that Beloved is the child she has lost" (p. 22). To support her realistic reading of Beloved, House cites W. E. B. Du Bois's volume *The Suppression of the African Slave-Trade to the United States of America, 1638–1870*, in which Du Bois notes that, despite the Congressional decree that banned any transportation of slaves to the U.S.A. after 1 January 1808, slaves continued to enter the country, especially during the decade leading up to the Civil War. House points out that the novel opens in 1873 and that given Beloved's presumed age, she could have been an African captured and transported illegally to the United States during the mid-1850s, the decade when most violations of the ban occurred, according to Du Bois.

In distinct contrast to House's realistic and historically informed reading of Beloved as a survivor of the Middle Passage, other scholars have interpreted Beloved's Middle Passage memories symbolically. For Deborah Horvitz, "Beloved stands for every African woman whose story will never be told. She is the haunting symbol of the many Beloveds – generations of mothers and daughters – hunted down and stolen from Africa" (p. 157). In Carol E. Henderson's reading of the novel, Beloved literally and symbolically "becomes the interior language of pain, externalized" (p. 94). Henderson points out that because of Beloved's physical presence as "a walking wound" (p. 91), she enables those around her to recognize their own wounds and to reclaim their scarred bodies and psyches – which is the first step of healing. Similar to Henderson, Karla Holloway reads Beloved's connection to immense suffering not only as devastating loss but as the possibility of healing:

> If Beloved is not only Sethe's dead daughter returned, but the return of all the faces, all the drowned, but remembered, faces of mothers and their children who have lost their being because of the force of . . . EuroAmerican slave-history, then she has become a cultural mooring place, a moment for reclamation and for renaming. (p. 522)

Because Beloved returns, she becomes associated not only with death, but with the possibility of remembering all those who have died. As a site of embodied memory, Beloved becomes "a cultural mooring place," in Holloway's view, where African American "spiritual histories" may be reclaimed (p. 523).

Ultimately, Beloved's interior monologue, with its vivid images and poetic prose, its rich possibilities and crucial ambiguities, seems to defy all scholarly attempts to affix one single interpretation to it. Valerie Smith in fact calls attention to these qualities in her reading of the novel, which leads toward a deconstructive thematic interpretation:

> One is tempted in reading her monologue to try to seek out referents, to figure out what, for example, "the hot thing" is that recurs throughout the section, why white men are called "the men without skin", what are "the sweet rocks" the men without skin bring to the black and angry dead. However, this section of the novel resists explication. It prompts, rather, the recognition that what is essentially and effectively unspoken can never be conveyed and comprehended linguistically. (1990, p. 352)

The ambiguity and inexplicability of Beloved's monologue are crucial in Smith's reading, for one of the aspects of Morrison's novel she finds so compelling is the struggle "to find a way to tell the story of the slave body in pain" (1990, p. 348) while at the same time recognizing "the unspeakability of the subject" (1990, p. 353). Smith identifies the central paradox of the novel as follows:

> By representing the inexpressibility of its subject, the novel asserts and reasserts the subjectivity of the former slaves and the depth of their suffering. The novel reminds us that our critical acumen and narrative capacities notwithstanding, we can never know what they endured. We can never enjoy a complacent understanding of lives lived under slavery. (1990, p. 354)

While in Part Two Beloved's return precipitates a reckoning with slavery and an important restoration of the bonds between black mothers and daughters that slavery severed, in Part Three, Beloved becomes greedy, insatiable, and vengeful. Once Sethe sees and touches the scar, she and Beloved become focused on each other, excluding Denver, first from their doting and games, then from their fierce arguments and fights. As Jean Wyatt notes, the line "you are mine" chanted by the women together in their interior monologues/trialogue foreshadows this turn of events: "'You are mine' is of course what the slave owners said, and as in the larger social order, the disregard of the other as subject, the appropriation of the other to one's own desires, leads to violence" (p. 482). Trudier Harris likewise emphasizes the destructive aspects of their bond by raising some tough questions: "Is ownership, ostensibly with love as its basis, any different from ownership by designation as chattel? Or are these women locked in a duel that is potentially more destructive than slavery?" (1990, p. 339). Indeed, it soon becomes clear that, despite all of Sethe's explanations, claims of love, and attempts to make up for the handsaw, Beloved cannot forgive or forget; she can assert only her own feelings of abandonment and pain. As Sethe withers away from trying to give Beloved anything and everything, Beloved grows bigger and bigger, symbolizing in part her unsatisfiable needs for a mother who will never leave her sight. Her desire for vengeance is also insatiable, for how can Sethe (or any mother) ever make up for that moment in the woodshed with the handsaw? Beloved makes claims for which there are no reparations.

What also becomes evident in Part Three of the novel is that whatever Beloved represents, it seems to be linked to the demonic. When the women gather and come to 124 to help Sethe, they see a "devil-child" that has "taken the shape of a pregnant woman" (p. 308). If Beloved is a young black woman who has escaped from white men who have been sexually exploiting her, then she might indeed be pregnant. Or she could be carrying Paul D's baby. But, clearly, there is something so dangerous about her need to punish Sethe that it seems otherworldly. Denver, for instance, understands quickly that she must get help for her mother when one day Sethe spits up "something she had not eaten" (p. 286), signifying the way that Beloved has begun to possess her body and soul. Trudier Harris's reading of the novel focuses on this aspect of Beloved's character, and Harris offers several terms to describe her frightening aspects: Beloved is "a witch, a ghost, a devil, or a succubus" (1991, p. 153). Harris further explains:

Like a vampire feeding vicariously, she becomes plump in direct proportion to Sethe's increasing gauntness. Vengeance is not the Lord's; it is Beloved's. Her very body becomes a manifestation of her desire for vengeance and of Sethe's guilt. She repays Sethe for her death, but the punishment is not quick or neat. (1991, p. 157)

Beloved's desire for vengeance by itself would wreak enough havoc, but Harris also points out that the sheer force of her desire is dangerous as well. "Pure desire" is a "destructive, irrational force," Harris observes, and adds: "It is out of desire for something that spirits are able to make the journey between the two worlds. Beloved, the personification of desire, thus epitomizes the demonic" (1991, p. 160). In Harris's reading, Beloved is a demon demanding vengeance, whose "brand of justice has no guiding morality to temper it with mercy" (1991, p. 160). Beloved's disappearance at the end of the novel, then, is a necessary departure that allows the human world of caring, love, and imagination to re-emerge.

Like Harris, Pamela Barnett focuses on the way that Beloved drains the energy of those around her. For Barnett, "Beloved is not just the ghost of Sethe's dead child; she is a succubus, a female demon and nightmare figure that sexually assaults male sleepers and drains them of semen" (p. 418). Barnett provocatively contends that Beloved rapes Paul D in the novel: she "collects sperm from Paul D to impregnate herself, then uses the life force of her mother's body to sustain her spawn" (p. 422). Draining vitality from Sethe, draining semen from Paul D, Beloved thus represents "the effects of institutionalized rape under slavery. When the enslaved persons" bodies were violated, their reproductive potential was commodified. The succubus, who rapes and steals semen, is metaphorically linked to such rapes and to the exploitation of African Americans" reproduction" (p. 419). For Barnett, Beloved "becomes an embodiment of the traumatic past and the embodied threat of that past's intrusion on the future" (p. 422). The community of women at the end cannot allow Beloved to deliver a child that would remind them of their own forced reproduction under slavery, and so they are motivated to find a way to exorcise her from Sethe's and their own lives. In Barnett's reading, Beloved's demonic qualities in the novel are necessary to command attention to historical atrocities, and yet she must be exorcised in order for a history of trauma to relinquish its hold and allow African Americans to go on living.

Beloved's disappearance among the women who are singing, during Sethe's attempt to attack Edward Bodwin with an ice pick and Denver's rush to prevent her mother from committing another killing, remains as enigmatic as her appearance in the novel. As the ghost of the daughter Sethe killed in 1855, Beloved cannot bear the sight of her mother abandoning her once again. As a survivor of the Middle Passage, she cannot help but see Edward Bodwin, whip in hand, as one of the men without skin who hurt her and others on the ship. As a "devil-child" symbolizing vengeance and desire, she is no match for the community of black women who have decided to gather Sethe into their midst again after 18 years of alienation. No matter how or why Beloved disappears in the end, the last two-page section of the novel, often referred to as a "coda" by Morrison scholars, is designed to haunt readers with the traces of Beloved's disappearance and erasure from memory. For Linda Krumholz, Beloved is not only Sethe's baby girl returned from the dead; she is not only Sethe's, Paul D's, and Denver's "ghost," representing the return of the repressed past: she is also "the reader's ghost, forcing us to face the historical past as a living and vindictive presence" (p. 115). Beloved, in Krumholz's view, functions as "the trickster of history" (p. 114), because even as she leads characters and readers "through a painful, emotional healing process," she also leaves them "with a haunting sense of the depth of pain and shame suffered in slavery" (p. 124).

To achieve this effect of both healing and haunting, Morrison's coda makes a double move: it insists that Beloved has been forgotten – that she is "disremembered and unaccounted for" (p. 323) – but it does so in such heightened lyrical and imagistic prose that the last pages ensure readers will not forget the importance of whatever Beloved signifies, or how important it is to Be-loved (to suggest yet another set of meanings embodied in her character). Following up on the inexplicable mysteriousness that surrounds Beloved throughout the novel and even in the coda, Avery F. Gordon connects Beloved to what cannot be represented or articulated: Beloved is both "the exceptional premise" of the novel and "a sign without a referent" (pp. 139, 178). As a ghost who haunts the living and who is haunted herself, Beloved speaks to the historical aporias of the Middle Passage and of slavery that cannot be recovered or known, no matter how much research or imagination tries to fill these absences. Thus Beloved's role as a "ghostly haunt" for Gordon lies in her ability to signify what is missing: "Something is happening you hadn't expected. . . . Something is making an appearance to you that had been kept from view" (pp. 178–9). Even after Beloved has been exorcised from the community, the haunting continues, as Gordon points out by citing the last section of the novel. "To be haunted is to be tied to historical and social effects" (p. 190), Gordon insists, and so the end of the novel tellingly reminds readers of secrets almost heard, of footsteps almost seen, of traces that may not be entirely visible but nonetheless require recognition. Beloved marks that space.

This chapter has demonstrated that Morrison's depiction of Beloved is so enigmatic and compelling that scholars have employed a wide range of theories to explicate her significance in the novel. Psychoanalytic approaches illuminate the seething desire that bubbles up through the novel in Beloved's insatiable appetites and in her possessive longing for Sethe. Psychoanalysis also provides insight into Denver's and Sethe's desire for what Beloved represents, and into the complexities of memory and forgetting that drive the novel. Black feminist theory examines the ways that gender, as well as race, shape Beloved's character and symbolic potential. An African American cultural studies approach highlights the folkloric aspects of Beloved, how she can be linked to certain African beliefs in the spirit world and afterlife as well as to African American oral tradition about spirits and demons. Historicism is also necessary for analyzing Beloved's role in the novel, particularly how she comes to signify the brutalities slave women experienced, and the traumatic, unrecorded experience of the Middle Passage. Deconstructive reading methodologies offer yet another layer of complexity to what Beloved might represent: as a repository of elusive, ineffable experiences, Beloved is the site where absence is made visible, where silence is voiced. In its attentiveness to the places where language begins to speak in slippages and aporias, deconstruction can usefully illuminate Beloved's role in standing in for what is ultimately unrepresentable and unspeakable.

Is Beloved a ghostly reincarnation of Sethe's murdered baby girl? Is she a flesh-and-blood young black woman who has been violated and abused, but is in fact not at all related to Sethe? Is she a literal survivor of the Middle Passage? Or should she be read primarily as a symbol, representing the ineffable and traumatic experience of the Middle Passage, or repressed histories, or insatiable (primal, primary) desire? Readers of the novel need as many perspectives as possible to tease out these haunting questions.

QUESTIONS FOR FURTHER ANALYSIS

1. Professor Scott Bradfield has written an essay provocatively titled "Why I Hate Toni Morrison's *Beloved*," in which he objects to, among other things, the depiction of Beloved as a character:

   > The book starts off really well; the central character of Sethe, and the haunting of her family, is strange and surprising and beautifully written; but the book never recovers from the arrival of the mysterious ghost-girl. I lose sight of Sethe; and the succubus doesn't work for me at all – some of the passages told through her eyes strike me as sentimental and phony, like beat poetry. (p. 94)

   Choose two or three incidents focusing on Beloved's perspective in the novel, and identify the kinds of rhetorical, linguistic, and aesthetic strategies Morrison employs to shape her readers" responses to Beloved. Keeping this analysis in mind, would you primarily agree or disagree with Bradfield's position?

2. One of the classic texts that Morrison likes to signify on in her

novels is the Bible. In fact, the epigraph for *Beloved* comes from Romans 9:25:

I will call them my people,
which were not my people;
and her beloved,
which was not beloved.

Consider how this biblical verse might be connected to Morrison's novel. Does it add yet another layer to the range of meanings Beloved comes to symbolize in the novel? Which of the scholarly interpretations discussed in this chapter might be helpful for analyzing the epigraph and its implications?

CHAPTER 4

RECONSTRUCTING BLACK MANHOOD

Some critics contend that Toni Morrison is much more attentive to the plight of African American women in *Beloved* than to the plight of black men. But April Lidinsky points out that, "while most critics have emphasized the matrilineal connections in *Beloved*, Morrison's text is also richly suggestive with regard to the various effects of slavery's disciplinary tactics on *masculinity*" (p. 202). In fact, Morrison's novel offers a complex and historically informed depiction of the constraints that slavery placed upon the desires, roles, and experiences of African American men. This chapter offers a close examination of Stamp Paid, Sixo, Halle, and Paul D, in particular, to reveal how the identity and selfhood of black men were shaped by slavery and its after-effects.

As historians have shown, and as the discussion of mothers and daughters in Chapter Two suggests, slavery disrupted family structures, relations, and roles. Black men under slavery found being a husband and a father in any autonomous sense to be difficult to say the least, and often impossible. White masters and slaveowners could force the break-up of family units by selling fathers, mothers, or children at any moment. They typically prohibited marriage between enslaved black men and women. White masters and slaveowners could, and often did, decide to exploit black women for their own needs, thus disrupting marital and conjugal bonds. Under the slave system, as Hortense Spillers reminds us:

'Family", as we practice and understand it "in the West" – the *vertical* transfer of a bloodline, of a patronymic, of titles and entitlements, of real estate and the prerogatives of "cold cash", from *fathers* to *sons* and in the supposedly free exchange of affectional ties between a male and a female of *his* choice – becomes the mythically revered privilege of a free and freed community. (p. 74)

These privileges were not open to black men under slavery. In fact, given the severe constraints the system of slavery placed upon black men, we might wonder how, or if, they could preserve any sense of themselves as autonomous individuals, as men, as lovers and husbands, as fathers, and as sons. This fraught psychological space is examined and dramatized in Morrison's *Beloved*.

As Pamela Barnett observes, the black male characters in *Beloved* find that slavery renders them "powerless and ostensibly passive," and they tend to explain their powerlessness as "emasculating" (p. 424). It is also worth noting that Sixo, Halle, Stamp Paid, and Paul D represent various models of black manhood under siege. All of them experience the demeaning and soul-numbing violence of slavery, but Sixo and Halle do not escape from slavery, while Stamp Paid and Paul D survive to face the difficulties of reconstructing a sense of black manhood after emancipation. By presenting readers with four models of black manhood, Morrison's novel depicts a range of possible reactions to the violence of slavery.

Sixo is especially significant, for he is the only one of the male slaves held at Sweet Home who continually resists the slave system's demeaning and dehumanizing effects. Sixo defies regulations prohibiting language, desire, mobility, and autonomous decision-making. While the typical brutalities of slavery were softened by Mr. Garner, the original owner of Sweet Home, once he dies and schoolteacher takes over the administration of the house and fields, Sweet Home becomes a place of severe discipline. During schoolteacher's rule, Sixo becomes openly defiant and is punished on several occasions. In one instance, Sixo, rather than remain racked with hunger, takes a pig, butchers it, roasts it, and feeds himself. When schoolteacher accuses him of stealing, Sixo denies the accusation, asserts his own description of his actions as "Improving your property, sir," and offers this explanation: "Sixo plant rye to give the high piece a better chance. Sixo take and feed the soil, give you more crop. Sixo take and feed Sixo give you more work" (p. 224). Sixo is able to use the racist logic of slaveowners, that slaves are not persons but property, to resist schoolteacher's accusations rhetorically at least; but he cannot escape schoolteacher's power to punish him physically: "schoolteacher beat him anyway to show him that definitions belong to the definers – not the defined" (p. 225).

Tellingly, Sixo's appearance is distinct among the slaves at Sweet Home – he is "Indigo with a flame-red tongue" (p. 25) – and Paul D remembers that at some point Sixo "stopped speaking English because there was no future in it" (p. 30), suggesting that Sixo returns to speaking his original African language. It is not just coincidental that Morrison depicts Sixo as more closely connected to his African origins than the other black slaves at Sweet Home, for it is his memory of this time before slavery that fuels his resistance. Disallowed from leaving Sweet Home on his own, Sixo nonetheless plans a way to meet Patsy, his lover, despite the lengthy journey involved (34 miles). His connection to ancestral spirits is made clear when he finds a place where they can consummate their love, but first asks the spirit of the original occupants of the land – the "Redmen's Presence" (p. 29) – for permission.

His integrity and autonomy become most dramatically apparent when Paul D, Sixo, and Patsy are caught by schoolteacher and a group of whitemen at the moment they plan to escape Sweet Home: Sixo pushes the Thirty-Mile woman so she will run away, and he distracts the white men by grabbing a rifle. Then he begins to sing his own song, so openly and defiantly, they become unnerved and use the rifle to knock him unconscious. When Sixo comes to, he has been placed on a roaring fire so that he will suffer and die before their eyes. But again his reaction shocks the white men: Sixo begins to engage in wild, defiant laughter and to call out, "Seven-O! Seven-O!" (p. 267), alluding to the fact that Patsy is pregnant, she has escaped, and his spirit will live on in their child. Trudier Harris argues that Sixo's "spirit cannot be conquered even if his body is destroyed. He is the ultimate man" (1991, p. 179). Indeed, the whitemen have to "shoot him to shut

him up" while he is being burned alive (p. 267), and Paul D under-
stands why, for Sixo voices a "hatred so loose it was juba" (p. 268).
(Juba refers to a rhythmic, celebratory dance originating in West
Africa that continued among slave communities in the U.S.A.)
Yvonne Atkinson calls attention to Morrison's phrasing here:
"The juxtaposition of *hatred* and *juba* creates such a dichotomy
that it establishes a dynamic image of hatred so unbounded that it
is a joyous happening, rancor unleashed" (p. 28).

If Sixo is a model of defiant black manhood, then Halle depicts
the vulnerability of the slave who tries to follow all the rules but
ends up suffering cruelly anyway. Under the ownership of the
Garners, Halle has been given enormous latitude: like all the other
slaves at Sweet Home, he works sunup to sundown, Monday
through Saturday; but on Sunday, his day of rest, he is allowed to
hire himself out to other plantations and earn money to be used
for buying his mother, Baby Suggs, out of slavery. He also woos
Sethe, and they are allowed to have a marriage ceremony of sorts.
They have three children together at Sweet Home, and none of
those children is sold away. But when schoolteacher takes the place
of Mr. Garner, circumstances change for Halle. He is no longer
allowed to work his "extra" anywhere other than at Sweet Home,
and so he has no way to finish paying off the debt he still owes for
his mother's freedom or to earn money to buy the rest of his family
out of slavery. He relates his concern to Sethe in a pointed question: "If all my labor is Sweet Home, including the extra, what I
got left to sell?" (p. 232). Schoolteacher also insinuates that he has
a better idea about how to make money via Halle's "extra" – either
by selling the children when they are a bit older, or by selling Halle
himself. This jagged reminder of the economics and the racist
logic of slavery provokes Halle into joining Sixo's plan to escape
Sweet Home, and when the plan goes awry, Halle is shattered. Paul
D suspects schoolteacher encountered Halle at a critical moment,
noticing his lack of subordination: maybe "schoolteacher heard a
tint of anxiety in his voice – the tint that would make him pick up
his ever-ready shotgun. Maybe Halle made the mistake of saying
"my wife" in some way that would put a light in schoolteacher's
eye" (p. 264). Whatever the case, Halle does not show up for the
escape attempt, and Sethe believes he has abandoned her. This

missed connection dramatizes the fragility of all familial relations under slavery, and the tenuousness of a husband's and father's ability to protect his family.

In his well-known study of the resourcefulness black people exercised under slavery, *Roll, Jordan, Roll: The World the Slaves Made*, historian Eugene D. Genovese identifies how the specific power dynamics of slavery impinged on black men's ability to carry out masculine, husbandly, and fatherly roles:

> The slaveholders deprived black men of the role of provider; refused to dignify their marriages or legitimize their issue; compelled them to submit to physical abuse in the presence of their women and children; made them choose between remaining silent while their wives and daughters were raped or seduced and risking death; and threatened them with separations from their family at any moment. (p. 490)

While Mr. Garner is the master of Sweet Home, Halle escapes the typical abuses of slavery that Genovese describes here. But under schoolteacher's watch, perhaps the worst of all happens: Halle is forced to watch silently while schoolteacher's nephews hold Sethe down and steal her milk (an equivalent to rape). Paul D is the last one to see Halle alive at Sweet Home, and he is devastated by what he witnesses: Halle sitting by a churn, smearing clabber (thickened milk or butter) all over his face. At that moment in 1855, Paul D did not know what could have rocked Halle to such a degree; it is not until he finds Sethe years later, in 1873, and she tells him about the incident that Paul D realizes that Halle must have witnessed the violation, and it was so traumatic "that day broke him like a twig" (p. 81). Sethe can hardly believe this revelation because it unsettles her vision of Halle as a strong man, who would do anything to protect and take care of his family. Recognizing Sethe's shock and disbelief, Paul D feels it necessary to point out that black men are vulnerable to being wounded deeply, though perhaps not in visible ways: "A man ain't a goddamn ax. Chopping, hacking, busting every goddamn minute of the day. Things get to him. Things he can't chop down because they're inside" (p. 81). What is also useful to note is that

Paul D's revealing look into Halle's vulnerability says as much about himself as it does about Halle.

In response to some readers" surprise that a man as strong as Halle suffers such a devastating breakdown in the novel, Morrison explains:

> Well, that's the carnage. It can't be abstract. The loss of that man to his mother, to his wife, to his children, to his friends, is a serious loss and the reader has to feel it, you can't feel it if he's in there. He has to *not* be there. (1988, p. 250)

Halle and Sixo do not escape the confines of Sweet Home and the violence of slavery, and readers feel keenly their loss each time they are subsequently remembered in the novel. Through their loss, Morrison's novel depicts the sheer terror and the brutal effects of slavery on black men.

Through the characters of Stamp Paid and Paul D, who witness the worst of slavery and live through it, Morrison's novel reveals the difficult struggle to reconstruct an affirmative sense of black manhood in slavery's wake. Stamp Paid is a crucial character in the novel in this regard: he is the voice of principle and the voice of justice; he uses his own life experiences and wisdom to teach Paul D about how to live with this burden; and he shapes the black community around him, urging them to look out for each other. But Stamp has paid dearly to reach this position of wisdom and insight. He tells Paul D about how he got his name: in slavery, he was called Joshua and had a wife named Vashti, who was forced into a sexual relationship with the master's son. The relationship goes on for about a year, with Vashti spending every night with the young master and Joshua not touching her, until one day Joshua decides to reveal the liaison subtly to the young master's wife by referring to a cameo the master has given Vashti. Soon afterward, the relationship is ended, Vashti returns to Joshua on a Sunday and says simply, "I'm back" (p. 275), and Joshua finds he wants to snap her neck, a long suppressed reaction to his feelings of disempowerment and betrayal. But instead of breaking Vashti's neck or harming himself – which would after all be taking out his frustrations on the wrong party, on the victims and not the victimizer, Joshua changes his name to "Stamp Paid" and decided after this, "he didn't owe anybody anything" (p. 218).

Stamp Paid subsequently discovers how much satisfaction he derives from helping other black people to deal with and survive their own kinds of misery. He becomes part of the Underground Railroad and helps Sethe and her baby find safe haven in Ohio after fleeing Sweet Home. Working together with Baby Suggs, John and Ella, and the black church, Stamp Paid helps to forge a black community where people look out for one another. His vision of community is sorely tested, though, when schoolteacher comes with slave catchers to reclaim Sethe and her children and none of the neighbors warns them, putting into motion a chain of events that leads to Sethe's act of desperate motherlove. Years later, Stamp Paid still cannot understand or come to terms with what he considers the "meanness" "that let them stand aside" and not make any attempt at a warning (p. 185), and the horrors of that day still run vividly through his mind. It is not at all clear why Stamp Paid decides to tell Paul D about this part of Sethe's past just when Paul D seems to have settled into a life with Sethe that might have a future. Does he see himself as offering a warning to Paul D in such a way as to undo the silence, the lack of warning, from that fateful day in 1855? Does he know that Paul D has rashly suggested to Sethe that they have a child together, and does he feel obligated to let Paul D know what kind of mother Sethe has been in the past? Does he want to tell Paul D in order to share some of the burden of his own memories of that day? Whatever the case, Stamp Paid finds himself unable to tell Paul D directly about the incident that he comes to call simply "the Misery'; instead he reads aloud a newspaper clipping reporting Sethe's infanticide, and all Paul D can say in response is, "That ain't her mouth" (p. 181), as he ponders the accompanying portrait.

This moment of the novel echoes Morrison's well-known essay about "unspeakable things unspoken," as Stamp Paid subsequently wonders, "How did information that had been in the newspaper become a secret that needed to be whispered in a pig yard?" (p. 199). Through the inner reflections of Stamp Paid and other characters, Morrison's novel frames an important consideration of how traumatic events – such as the degradation, racism, and violence of the slave system and its aftermath – can lead to silence and forgetting. Sometimes events become unspoken because no one will discuss them; other times, events become unspeakable because there are no words and sentences that can adequately articulate them. Stamp Paid finds himself unable to tell his own story of what happened on the day when Sethe killed her own child. And though he comes to regret his role in breaking up Paul D's and Sethe's relationship by sharing the news story, he cannot summon up the will to knock on Sethe's door to see how she is taking the loss. Six days in a row he steps onto her porch and up to her door, but cannot bring himself to knock. It is only after he recognizes how badly he had judged Baby Suggs's reaction to the Misery – her loss of heart and faith, her decision to remain in bed and give up on everything – that he finds the will to return to Sethe's porch. And he reaches that understanding by surveying the miseries of black people in his present moment:

> Eighteen seventy-four and whitefolks were still on the loose. Whole towns wiped clean of Negroes; eighty-seven lynchings in one year alone in Kentucky; four colored schools burned to the ground; grown men whipped like children; children whipped like adults; black women raped by the crew; property taken, necks broken. He smelled skin, skin and hot blood. The skin was one thing, but human blood cooked in a lynch fire was a whole other thing. The stench stank. (p. 212)

Stamp Paid becomes a witness to the cruelties and horrors that continue for black people even in a post-slavery era, and he can hardly find words to convey adequately the terror of it all. "The stench stank": the deliberate repetition here signals the failure of words to communicate the way in which this knowledge rocks him.

But even more harrowing is the ribbon that he finds while tying up his boat along a river bank. He glimpses something red attached to the ribbon, which he initially thinks might be a feather from a cardinal. But as he picks it up, he discovers that "what came loose in his hand was a red ribbon knotted around a curl of wet woolly hair, clinging still to its bit of scalp" (pp. 212–13). Dropping the curl of hair to the ground, Stamp puts the ribbon in his pocket and tries to walk home as usual. But he finds himself dizzy and breathless, and when he is forced to stop and rest, he allows himself to express some of his pent-up feelings about the cruelty and violence whitefolks are capable of: "What *are* these people? You tell me, Jesus. What *are* they?" (p. 213). At that moment, Stamp Paid comes to understand how Baby Suggs could have been utterly undone by the threat of white violence. And so fingering the red ribbon in his pocket, he finally brings himself to knock on Sethe's door. Although Sethe does not answer, it is enough for Stamp Paid to hear the roaring voices from inside, which he understands as "the people of the broken necks, of fire-cooked blood and black girls who had lost their ribbons" (p. 213) clamoring to be heard. Once he hears this roar, he begins to take action to figure out how to help Sethe, how to look out for Denver, and how to support Paul D.

Stamp Paid's ability to face the brutalities of slavery and the racist violence of the Reconstruction Era, his enduring concern for black people's individual and collective survival and well-being, along with the ability to reflect critically on his own motives and actions, make him an ideal representation of black manhood in the novel. In *Beloved*, black manhood in its positive manifestations is not rigidly patriarchal and authoritarian; rather, black manhood embodies both strength and humility, leadership and vulnerability – indeed, these critical contradictions are essential for the fullest and most productive expression of black manhood.

Stamp Paid is a doer, a man of action. It is important to note that Morrison's novel offers a different vision of black manhood in Paul D, who is much more introspective than Stamp. Paul D has been one of a similarly named group of brothers at Sweet Home: Paul A, Paul F, and Paul D. Lacking a distinct first name, and thus signifying the dehumanizing practices of slavery, Paul D embodies a fraught sense of selfhood that arises out of these conditions and that is put under scrutiny throughout the novel. Paul D continually reflects on what it means for him, for anyone, to be a black man, and throughout the novel he asks more penetrating questions than he finds satisfying answers.

In contrast to Stamp Paid, Paul D has spent most of the years after fleeing from slavery on the run or on the move; hence, he has not had the familial or community ties that might provide him with models or support for re-inventing himself as a free black man. He has had traumatic, formative experiences at Sweet Home and in Alfred, Georgia, that influence his behavior and attitudes when he finds Sethe in 1873 in Cincinnati and begins to reconnect with her, but he does not (or cannot bear to) think about these experiences most of the time. As Cheryl A. Wall rightly observes: "Paul D is surely the novel's most reluctant story-teller. He has deliberately locked the people, the places, and the images that could trigger his memories in a tin box" (p. 102). His experiences, however, have shaped him in intangible ways so that he functions as a sympathetic ear for women he encounters: "Not even trying, he had become the kind of man who could walk into a house and make the women cry. . . . There was something blessed in his manner. Woman saw him and wanted to weep . . . and told him things they only told each other" (p. 20). This description suggests that there is a crucial gender ambiguity about Paul D; in some capacity, he serves a feminine, womanly, role for these women. So Paul D is not surprised to find that soon after entering 124 Bluestone Road, Denver has a fit of weeping and Sethe reveals a harrowing intimate story about how she got the tree on her back.

Paul D is not only a man so gentle and empathetic that he seems womanly at times, he is also a man who acts authorita-tively, even rashly at other times. When Paul D enters Sethe's house and encounters the red light and strong vibrations of the ghost, his first impulse is to throw furniture around and break up the house to force the spirit to leave. He does not think twice about assuming the role as the man of a house that he has just entered. He also dreams of being Sethe's lover and of creating a family together with himself as the head, a desire signified by the way he, Sethe, and Denver hold hands as a unit on their way back from a day at a local carnival. This is the precise moment when Beloved enters the novel, not only to resurrect the past trauma that no one has wanted to think about, not only to reclaim and punish her mother, but also to push Paul D out of his unexamined assumptions about manhood as a position of always being in control, taking decisive action, suppressing emotion and weakness, and existing in certainty. When Beloved begins to summon Paul D to her, he cannot help but go; when Beloved raises her skirts, he cannot stop himself from coupling with her. In short, Beloved's control over Paul D undoes his sense of manhood: "Because he was a man and a man could do what he would . . . And it was he, *that* man, who had walked from Georgia to Delaware, who could not go or stay put where he wanted to in 124 – shame" (p. 148).

Pamela Barnett goes so far as to suggest that Beloved rapes Paul D and that this reversal of the typical rape scenario – making the woman the perpetrator and the man the victim – makes Paul D's story of the rape unspeakable (p. 424). Certainly, Paul D seems unable to comprehend fully what Beloved does to him; the closest he comes is to think to himself, "I am not a man" (p. 151). He is also at a loss to explain his behavior and anxiety to Sethe, and instead says, "I want you pregnant, Sethe. Would you do that for me?" At the same moment, he realizes that her pregnancy would be a solution to a number of problems: it would be "a way to hold on to her [Sethe], document his manhood and break out of the girl's [Beloved's] spell – all in one" (p. 151).

Beloved's discomforting manipulation of Paul D leads to fissures in his ideas of gender and selfhood. When Stamp Paid shows him the news clipping reporting Sethe's infanticide and trial, Paul D is thrown into radical uncertainty about Sethe and, by extension, about the possibility of truly knowing another human being, himself included. He tries to ward off this uncertainty by resorting to simplistic ideas of what makes a person human in the halting conversation he and Sethe have about what happened the day schoolteacher came to reclaim his so-called property. While Sethe seeks to tell the events of that day from her own perspective, emphasizing her motherlove, Paul D listens with a lack of sympathy or real understanding. He cuts Sethe to the bone when he admonishes her with "You got two feet, Sethe, not four" (p. 194), and then walks out on her.

Moved first by Beloved, then removing himself from Sethe's house, Paul D becomes literally, socially, and psychologically displaced. This displacement allows him to become unmoored from normative ideas of selfhood, gender, and sexuality, and he allows himself to remember and reflect on how he came to believe what a man is (and is not). As Deborah Ayer Sitter notes, Paul D thinks of Sixo as the ideal man, but Sixo in fact is a model of African manhood, which is not available to Paul D (p. 23); so he takes his ideas of manliness from Mr. Garner's pronouncements, which are necessarily rooted in white male privilege and assumptions (p. 24). One of the unusual aspects of Sweet Home as it was operated by Mr. Garner is that the black male slaves were regarded as "men," meaning they were "allowed" and "encouraged to correct Garner," even to "defy him," Paul D remembers, and adds: "To invent ways of doing things; to see what was needed and attack it without permission. To buy a mother, choose a horse or a wife, handle guns, even learn reading if they wanted to" (p. 147). Under Garner's seemingly benevolent version of slavery, Paul D has no reason to question his identity or manhood. But when Garner dies and schoolteacher takes his place, the rules become very different, and Paul D is given an education in subordination, humiliation, and degradation to learn his proper place in the slave system, and so to learn that he is not a man, but a commodity akin to an animal or piece of property that a white man can buy and sell as he pleases.

It is schoolteacher's discipline after the failed escape attempt that wounds Paul D most deeply as he watches Sixo die, sees Halle lose his mind, and never finds out what has become of his brother Paul A. For trying to escape, Paul D has his legs chained, and a collar with three lengthy spokes (his "neck jewelry" as he calls it (p. 269)) is placed around his neck so that he cannot do any simple function, such as eating or sleeping, without being constantly reminded of his place. Then the day after his escape attempt, "the bit" (p. 84) is placed in Paul D's mouth, not only to cause immense physical pain but to teach him the cruelest lesson of all: that he is nothing more than a piece of livestock – like a horse that is trained to accept a rider, he has no self, no autonomous will, no voice. But as Paul D reveals this incident to Sethe, it is not the bit itself that causes the most psychological and soul-wounding damage; it is the sight of a rooster named Mister, strutting around the yard, looking "free. Better than me":

> Mister was allowed to be and stay what he was. But I wasn't allowed to be and stay what I was. . . . Schoolteacher changed me. I was something else and that something was less than a chicken sitting in the sun on a tub. (p. 86)

Responding to this scene in Morrison's novel, Philip M. Weinstein raises an ominous question: "Unable to be a Mister, how does an unpropertied black male negotiate his manhood?" (p. 94). Paul D searches for answers to this question throughout *Beloved*.

Schoolteacher's disciplinary practices at Sweet Home begin to challenge Paul D's conceptions of himself as a worthy individual, as an autonomous human being, and as a black man. Paul D's subsequent experiences on a chain gang in Alfred, Georgia, call into question ideas of black manhood and sexual desire. At the prison camp, Paul D joins a coffle of 46 black men, who are chained together to perform manual labor from dawn to dusk and who sleep in cages located in a deep trench every night. Perhaps the most harrowing aspect of the coffle, however, is the sexual abuse the black men are forced to endure from the white guards every morning before work begins. Lee Edelman notes the "connections among racism, castration, and homosexuality" this scene brings to the forefront (p. 59). Highlighting the fact that the white guards force the black prisoners to kneel in front of them while they perform fellatio, Edelman argues that, in effect, the black men are symbolically emasculated and castrated in this scenario (pp. 54–5). Edelman further suggests that "the guards homophobically terrorize their prisoners with the prospect of compulsory inscription in the position of the 'homosexual', or more precisely, the position of the 'faggot'" (p. 56).

In order to survive this nightmare, the men of the coffle must relinquish ideas of black identity, manhood, and sexuality. As prisoners, they are continually subjected to the orders and whims of the guards. Through their sexual abuse, they are forced into a feminine position of being vulnerable, victimized, and raped.

And because this sexual violation is male on male, they are forced into a state of abjection, viewing their own sexual position as that of the "faggot." As symbolized in the heavy chain that links the ankle bracelet of all prisoners together, they must learn to think of themselves *not* as individual men with their own autonomous will and desire, but rather as a collective entity in which, if one man falls or attacks a guard, all of them will surely suffer dire consequences. Yet out of this forced collectivity the novel demonstrates that resistance is possible. Not only do the prisoners create a community in the midst of crisis, but as Carol E. Henderson points out, they create "an alternative system of speech that . . . reclaim[s] their body as voice" (pp. 106–7). They develop a communication system utilizing gesture, song, and the vibrations of the chain – all of which enables them to escape the trench en masse when heavy rains threaten to create a river of mud that would bury them alive. April Lidinsky astutely notes that they transform the chain, "the very device that keeps them partitioned[,] into a mechanism for collective agency" (p. 204).

As Paul D's story unfolds in the novel, his experiences of being abused and violated in Alfred, Georgia, become interwoven with his experience of being summoned against his will by Beloved: in fact, his memories of the prison camp are narrated right before the section in which Beloved "moves" him for the first time. How are these episodes connected? First, both force Paul D to question his received ideas of manhood. As Pamela Barnett points out, Paul D is "the only principal character who must deal with two forced sexual encounters'; he experiences homosexual rape on the coffle and heterosexual rape later on with Beloved, violations that lead to "constant meditation on the meaning of his manhood" (p. 423). This is true enough: and yet the novel adds another layer of complexity in suggesting that his relationship with Beloved helps Paul D undo some of the damage Alfred, Georgia, inflicted on him. In order to survive the traumas of the past, Paul D has learned to repress any feeling, emotion, or desire: he has a "tobacco tin buried in his chest where a red heart used to be" (p. 86) that stays rusted shut – until he is moved by Beloved. Notably, in their initial sexual encounter, Paul D begins to shout out "Red heart. Red heart" (p. 138) again and again, as their illicit coupling tears open the lid of his tobacco tin, breaks some of the silences that have allowed his traumatic experiences to go unspoken, and opens him up to deep feelings. The interpretation of Paul D's and Beloved's relationship is debatable and significant in its implications: while Barnett insists unequivocally that Beloved rapes Paul D, Valerie Smith argues that "the act of intercourse with Beloved restores Paul D to himself, restores his heart to him" (1990, p. 348). Clearly this is a textual moment allowing for a wide range of interpretation.

As Paul D begins to reckon with the implications of his experiences, as he begins to scrutinize himself and admit to weaknesses, he becomes an affirmative model for the reconstruction of black manhood. This development is best seen late in the novel when he returns to his memories of Sweet Home under Garner and schoolteacher, and begins to pinpoint the political and structural forces that have left him and other black men uncertain of how to be truly free:

> For years Paul D believed schoolteacher broke into children what Garner had raised into men. . . . Now, plagued by the contents of his tobacco tin, he wondered how much difference there really was between before schoolteacher and after. Garner called and announced them men – but only on Sweet Home, and by his leave. Was he naming what he saw or creating what he did not? That was the wonder of Sixo, and even Halle; it was always clear to Paul D that those two were men whether Garner said so or not. It troubled him that, concerning his own manhood, he could not satisfy himself on that point. Oh, he did manly things, but was that Garner's gift or his own will? (p. 260)

Asking the necessary question of where manhood comes from allows Paul D to break free, to accept the responsibility for shaping a concept of black manhood that will allow him to create a "livable life" and to be connected to Sethe, to Stamp Paid, and to other members of the black community.

It is a reborn Paul D who returns to 124 at the end of the novel, not to count Sethe's feet but to rub them. He is able to look after

Sethe's well-being at the end because he has come to understand black manhood not as rooted in authority and patriarchy, but as being strong enough to express tenderness and compassion. He has been influenced by resurfacing memories of Sixo describing his feelings for the Thirty-Mile Woman: "She is a friend of my mind. She gather me, man. The pieces I am, she gather them and give them back to me in all the right order. It's good, you know, when you got a woman who is a friend of your mind" (p. 321). This model for an intimate relationship between a black man and a black woman pushes to the side Paul D's earlier emphasis on his own sexual desire for Sethe. It recenters their relationship on mutuality and reciprocity, reflected in Paul D's overwhelming feelings for Sethe at the end: "He wants to put his story next to hers" (p. 322). As Deborah Ayer Sitter notes about this resonant line, "'Next to' speaks of equality – Sethe's story is as important as his. Unlike the hero's story – all ego, possession, and dominance – Paul D's story . . . comes to suggest 'a family relationship rather than a man's laying claim'" (p. 26).

Setting Paul D's and Sethe's stories side by side at the end of *Beloved* has another important implication as well: Morrison's novel is as interested in exploring the lives of black men as it is in revealing the lives of black women. Through the characters of Sixo, Halle, Stamp Paid, and Paul D, *Beloved* presents diverse and complex perspectives on black manhood. Paul D's journey is perhaps the most instructive since, despite the end of slavery, he has remained enslaved to disabling ideas of real manhood. Through his development as a character, *Beloved* suggests that the reconstruction of black manhood is a vital step in restoring the bonds severed by the slave system between black men, black women, their families, and their community.

QUESTIONS FOR FURTHER ANALYSIS

1. In her book *Self-Discovery and Authority in Afro-American Narrative*, Valerie Smith points out that slave narratives written by African American men tend to "mythologiz[e] rugged individuality, physical strength, and geographical mobility'; in other words, they "enshrine cultural definitions

of masculinity" (1987, p. 34). Smith then adds, "The plot of the standard narrative may thus be seen as not only the journey from slavery to freedom but also the journey from slavehood to manhood" (1987, p. 34). Consider how the depiction of the black male characters in Morrison's *Beloved* might compare to the typical plot of nineteenth-century slave narratives. Does Morrison's novel uphold this double journey into freedom and manhood, or call it into question? Why or why not?

2. The talented actor Denzel Washington was approached about playing the role of Paul D in the film version of *Beloved* that Oprah Winfrey produced and starred in (as Sethe). But Washington said he was not interested in the role because he "didn't like the character":

> He was walking around with his hat in his hand, bowing and scraping. Sleeps with Oprah and two minutes later he's sleeping with her daughter, who's a ghost. That ain't me. I said, "Get Danny [Glover] to do it. Danny'll do it". I'm not knocking him, but it wasn't for me. (Nelson 1997)

Part of Washington's objection seems to do with the strangeness of the story itself, involving potential incest and a ghostly presence. But another aspect of his rejection of the role might be linked to conceptions of black manhood: Washington did not want to portray a black man who appears "hat in his hand, bowing and scraping." Is Washington's description of Paul D as a character accurate for the movie? What about for the novel? If Toni Morrison were to respond directly to Denzel Washington's objections, what might she say to him about the novel's interest in black men and ideas of black manhood?

CHAPTER 5

WHITEFOLKS AND WHITENESS IN *BELOVED*

In Part One of *Beloved*, Sethe and Paul D are walking along a street when Paul D firmly grasps her elbow and they step off into the dirt to let "Four women, walking two abreast", pass by (p. 152). Morrison's narrative voice does not specify the race of the women they encounter, but their automatic response of stepping aside lets readers know these are white women. By not explicitly naming race, Morrison's novel calls attention to the operations of white privilege that are so entrenched they have come to seem natural or inevitable. Similarly, when Stamp Paid and Paul D are talking in the churchyard at the end of Part Two, an unidentified man rides up on a horse and asks them if they know where "a gal name of Judy" lives (p. 272). Again, race is unspecified, but careful readers will detect that the stranger is white. For one thing, Stamp immediately addresses the man as "sir," and for another, the stranger feels entitled to look down on Paul D taking a drink from a bottle and to deliver an unasked-for sermonette: "Look here. . . . There's a cross up there, so I guess this here's a church or used to be. Seems to me like you ought to show it some respect, you follow me?" (p. 273). Stamp immediately intervenes to say, "Yes, sir. . . . You right about that. That's just what I come over to talk to him about. Just that" (p. 273). In a trickster move, Stamp says what he knows the white man wants to hear and then goes right back to his real topic of conversation with Paul D.

Morrison has said in an interview that she wanted to write about these encounters without specifying race, without using "the traditional language of stereotype" (1989d, p. 265). She goes on to raise an interesting question: "can you think what it would mean for me and my relationship to language and to texts to be able to write without having to always specify to the reader the race of the characters?" (1989d, p. 266). It would be "liberating," she answers in response to her own question. Because of *Beloved*'s historical setting at a time in American history when the ideologies of slavery and miscegenation resulted in the "one-drop" rule of determining whether a person was black or white, there are not many opportunities for the kind of "liberating" moments that Morrison speaks of in her interview. But in the two incidents from *Beloved* discussed above, Morrison already drives a wedge in essentialist views of race based on skin color or blood quantum; unspoken whiteness in these scenes calls attention to the ways in which race typically goes unmarked for white people. Moreover, Morrison's handling of these encounters makes it very clear that whiteness is not a matter of skin color or blood; rather, it is a matter of ideology and privilege.

As a novel that interrogates the inhumanity and racism of the slave system, *Beloved* is certainly, as Babacar M'Baye insists, "a critique of the white American ideology of racial supremacy" (p. 181). *Beloved* also makes some bold moves to develop this critique. First, the novel remains centered on African American characters throughout, relegating white characters to the margins. In other words, while white masters may have had unquestionable political and social control during and after slavery, Morrison's novel counters by giving narrative control to her black characters. Second, while the number of white characters is limited in *Beloved*, the range of their ideological investment in whiteness is diverse, and it is thus valuable to examine the raced and racist assumptions that these characters make. This chapter discusses schoolteacher, the Garners, Mr. Edward Bodwin, and Amy Denver to analyze larger issues of what Morrison calls "whitefolks" (all one word) and whiteness in the novel.

In fact, one of the central questions Sethe, Paul D, Baby Suggs, and Stamp Paid consider is whether all white people should be lumped together in a category like "whitefolks." Sethe insists in a couple of key instances on making distinctions among individuals and in believing that "for every schoolteacher there would be an Amy" (p. 222). Denver is trying to figure out this issue for herself late in the novel when she recalls a fierce conversation between Sethe and Baby Suggs on the nature of white people:

> "They got me out of jail," Sethe once told Baby Suggs.
> "They also put you in it," she answered.
> "They drove you 'cross the river."
> "On my son's back."
> "They gave you this house."
> "Nobody *gave* me nothing."
> "I got a job from them."
> "He got a cook from them, girl."
> "Oh, some of them do all right by us."
> "And every time it's a surprise, ain't it?"
> "You didn't used to talk this way."
> "Don't box with me. There's more of us they drowned than there is all of them ever lived from the start of time. Lay down your sword. This ain't a battle; it's a rout." (p. 287)

Because of what Baby Suggs witnessed the day schoolteacher rode to 124 Bluestone – "they came in my yard," she repeats to Stamp Paid (p. 211) – she sees whitefolks as one destructive group: "Those white things have taken all I had or dreamed . . . and broke my heartstrings too. There is no bad luck in the world but whitefolks" (pp. 104–5). Baby is free on the north side of the Ohio River to contemplate the meaning of whitefolks, and what she sees clearly is a pervasive system of ignorance, racism, and violence. In Baby's words with Sethe, she tries to point to this larger system that makes it irrelevant if some white people are "good'; because white supremacist thinking is so entrenched and has such power, it is dangerous not to recognize the potential for violence in any cross-racial encounter, Baby tries to point out.

Baby Suggs's perspective resonates with the insightful comments about whiteness found in James Baldwin's essays (Morrison, in fact, selected the essays for the volume that Library of America published in 1998). Baldwin poignantly points to the dangers for blacks of thinking of white people as benevolent:

> Most Negroes cannot risk assuming that the humanity of white people is more real to them than their color. And this leads, imperceptibly but inevitably, to a state of mind in which, having long ago learned to expect the worst, one finds it very easy to believe the worst. The brutality with which Negroes are treated in this country simply cannot be overstated, however unwilling white men may be to hear it. (p. 326)

The brutality Baldwin speaks of here appears throughout Morrison's novel, but it is especially present in Stamp Paid's inner reflections on whitepeople. Finding the red ribbon attached to a curl of hair and a bit of scalp makes Stamp wonder, as discussed in the previous chapter, "What *are* these people? You tell me, Jesus. What *are* they?" (p. 213). His thoughts on this question lead him to an important insight about the nature of whiteness and racism:

> Whitepeople believed that whatever the manners, under every dark skin was a jungle. Swift unnavigable waters, swinging screaming baboons, sleeping snakes, red gums ready for their sweet white blood. In a way, he thought, they were right. The more coloredpeople spent their strength trying to convince them how gentle they were, how clever and loving, how human, the more they used themselves up to persuade whites of something Negroes believed could not be questioned, the deeper and more tangled the jungle grew inside. But it wasn't the jungle blacks brought with them to this place from the other (livable) place. It was the jungle whitefolks planted in them. And it grew. It spread. In, through and after life, it spread, until it invaded the whites who had made it. Touched them every one. Changed and altered them. Made them bloody, silly, worse than even they wanted to be, so scared were they of the jungle they had made. The screaming baboon lived under their own white skin; the red gums were their own. (p. 234)

What Stamp's thinking makes clear here is how much racism destroys the racist as well as the object of his or her derision.

Stamp's thoughts also trace the way in which the construction of civilization as white/American depends so intimately on defining the savage as black/African, a subject that Morrison explores at length in her study of American Africanisms in literature written by white authors, titled *Playing in the Dark*. Morrison has described this process of projection and differentiation on the basis of race as follows:

Africanism is the vehicle by which the American self knows itself as not enslaved, but free; not repulsive, but desirable; not helpless, but licensed and powerful; not history-less, but historical; not damned, but innocent; not a blind accident of evolution, but a progressive fulfillment of destiny. (1992b, p. 52)

Linking savagery to blackness becomes a necessary projection for white people so that they can be assured of their own status as gentle, civilized, and superior.

This way of thinking in the novel is best represented by schoolteacher. He looks appalled one day when Paul D and the others are playing "a pitching game" (p. 259), since the fact that slaves might play games and be sociable does not fit his ideas of blackness as the not-human. He beats Sixo for trying to outwit him, as discussed in the previous chapter, because definitions belong to white people and their superior thinking. He requires Sethe to make the ink that he uses to record measurements and observations in his notebook about the Sweet Home slaves; though readers are never privy to what this notebook contains, we can assume he is creating scientific records to justify his belief that whites are human and superior, and that black slaves are inferior in comparison, closer to chattel than humanity. As Mae G. Henderson observes, schoolteacher uses "a process of negative self-identification" to advance his own sense of superiority: "It is Sethe's 'savagery' which confirms Schoolteacher's 'civilization', her 'bestiality' which confirms his 'humanity'" (p. 70).

It is important to note precisely how schoolteacher's actions and beliefs affect Sethe. When she tries to explain to Beloved why killing kept her safe, it becomes clear that it is not the beatings or the whippings or the other acts of brutality that commence once schoolteacher comes to Sweet Home that precipitate Sethe's decision. It is the desire to keep her children out of schoolteacher's methods of white supremacist thinking and racist accounting: "No notebook for my babies and no measuring string neither" (p. 233), Sethe explains to Beloved in her mind. This declaration follows a memory that has bubbled up that Sethe never told anyone, about the day she overheard schoolteacher say her name and then listened in on his instructions to his nephews to write in their own notebooks properly: "No, no. That's not the way. I told you to put her human characteristics on the left; her animal ones on the right. And don't forget to line them up" (p. 228). Sethe has to ask Mrs. Garner what the word "characteristics" means, and she is told, "A characteristic is a feature. A thing that's natural to a thing" (p. 230). Armed with this definition, Sethe immediately grasps that schoolteacher represents the worst thing that could happen to her children – that is, to learn to see themselves as *naturally* inferior, savage, and not-human. Indeed, late in the novel, Sethe tries to justify her actions to Beloved in just this way. She tries to warn her that "anybody white could take your whole self for anything that came to mind. Not just work, kill, or maim you, but dirty you. Dirty you so bad you couldn't like yourself anymore. Dirty you so bad you forgot who you were" (p. 295). Sethe calls attention to the psychological and spiritual devastations of racism in her remarks. She goes on to add that, "though she and others lived through and got over it, she could never let it happen to her own. The best thing she was, was her children. Whites might dirty *her* all right, but not her best thing" (pp. 295–6). Sethe vows not to let her children be defined by an ideology that not only would beat them into submission but would break them in mind, heart, and soul.

Sethe's attempt to keep her children safe from schoolteacher's measurements and notebooks by killing them resonates with James Baldwin's observation that "the power of the white world is threatened whenever a black man refuses to accept the white world's definitions" (p. 326). Sethe emphasizes this point in her account of that day when she tells Paul D, "I stopped him . . . I took and put my babies where they'd be safe" (p. 193). Schoolteacher's view of her actions is quite different but revealing. When schoolteacher sees the dead child in the woodshed, he thinks, "But now she'd gone wild" (p. 176), which leads to his smug opinion that black slaves "needed every care and guidance in the world to keep them from the cannibal life they preferred" (p. 177). Schoolteacher relies on his ingrained ideas of race and white superiority to deflect any understanding of Sethe's desperate act. But the one nephew whom he has brought along is less secure and certain in his thinking; he seems to sense the implications of Sethe's killing, even if he does not quite understand them: "What she go and do that for? On account of a beating? Hell, he'd been beat a million times and he was white" (p. 176). The questions rolling through his mind include a puzzling reference to whiteness: does this signify a hope for reassurance that because he is white he would not ever do such a thing? In fact, no reassurance comes, and the questions continue: "But no beating ever made him . . . I mean no way he could have . . . What she go and do that for?" (pp. 176–7). The nephew's inability to finish his sentences suggests just how deeply Sethe's desperate act has shaken his way of looking at the world. He repeats the haunting question – "What she want to go and do that for?" – without any answer, suggesting that Sethe's actions defy the way she has been measured and accounted for in schoolteacher's notebook.

Schoolteacher is easily categorized as the most reprehensible white character in *Beloved*, and represents some of the worst qualities of typical Southern slaveowners. A recurring question in Morrison's novel is whether schoolteacher's cruel and dehumanizing methods should be distinguished from, or read as similar to, Mr. Garner's unorthodox, and perhaps even benign, methods and assumptions. Mr. Garner allowed his male slaves to use guns, to express their opinions, and to choose their own women, and Mr. Garner never slept with his female slaves. Schoolteacher, on the other hand, constantly asserts his authority and superiority through beatings and disciplinary apparatus, and also through intellect, as when he instructs his nephews to categorize Sethe by her animal and human characteristics. Garner considered the slaves to be "men'; schoolteacher considers them to be property or chattel. Interestingly, Sixo, unlike the other Sweet Home men, does not feel sorrow at the death of Mr. Garner, since in his eyes all whites, all slaveowners, are equally reprehensible – that is, until schoolteacher comes to Sweet Home and then, as Paul D remembers, Sixo "was mighty sorry; they all were" (p. 259). But Paul D himself wonders in retrospect how much difference there was before schoolteacher and after, and realizes that Garner controlled a lot of their lives through his benevolence. While Garner referred to his slaves as men, Paul D sees that "they were only Sweet Home men at Sweet Home. One step off that ground and they were trespassers among the human race" (pp. 147–8). Also, while Garner encouraged them to be inventive and self-directed as they worked, he never gave them the privilege of deciding not to work – only "of deciding how to" (p. 147).

Paul D's questioning of Garner's "good" treatment is echoed in a conversation Halle and Sethe previously had on the same subject. Sethe opens the conversation by saying about Mr. and Mrs. Garner, "they ain't like the whites I seen before. The ones in the big place I was before I came here." Sethe perhaps wants Halle to confirm her idea that the Garners are special, but instead he asks, "How these different?" When she replies, "they talk soft for one thing," he responds, "It don't matter, Sethe. What they say is the same. Loud or soft" (pp. 230–1). His attitude is echoed by Baby Suggs's experience. Baby recalls her first impressions of the Garners when they brought her from a Carolina plantation to Sweet Home as being mostly good: "Lillian Garner called her Jenny for some reason," Baby remembers, "but she never pushed, hit or called her mean names. Even when she slipped in cow dung and broke every egg in her apron, nobody said you-black-bitch-what's-the-matter-with-you and nobody knocked her down" (p. 164). While Baby is treated better physically at the Garners," she nonetheless understands she is still a slave: "It's better here, but I'm not" (p. 165). That during her 10 years of service to them the Garners never know the name she uses for herself – Baby Suggs – and instead call her Jenny (the name on her bill of sale) indicates the chasm between master and slave even under the most benign conditions.

This ignorance is tellingly reproduced in the encounters

various black characters have with the foremost anti-slavery, abolitionist figure in the novel, Mr. Edward Bodwin. Is it really a case of mistaken identity when Sethe rushes at him with an ice pick near the end of the novel, thinking he is schoolteacher returning to 124? Or is there very little substantive distinction between their social positions as white men enmeshed in a system of white supremacy and privilege? Avery F. Gordon describes Sethe's misrecognition of the two white men as "an insightful mistake" that calls attention to limits of Emancipation and abolitionism in achieving "real freedom, real emancipation" (p. 162). The novel calls attention to these limits in a variety of scenes and encounters that readers must scrutinize carefully. For example, when Mr. Garner takes Baby Suggs to the Bodwins" house in Cincinnati so that they can help her settle into life as a free black woman, they tell her directly, "We don't hold with slavery, even Garner's kind" (p. 171). While it is true they offer her a place to live, it is also the case that they demand a significant amount of work as recompense: "In return for laundry, some seamstress work, a little canning and so on (oh shoes, too), they would permit her to stay there. Provided she was clean. The past parcel of colored wasn't" (p. 171). These extra stipulations call into question their attitudes toward blacks, suggesting that abolitionists are not free from perpetuating disabling stereotypes.

This issue is corroborated when Denver makes her own sojourn to the Bodwins" house in Cincinnati to ask for help. When Janey, a black servant, suggests that Denver might be able to stay and look after the Bodwins at night, their conversation moves onto a discussion of "whitefolks":

What did Denver have to do at night?
"Be here. In case."
In case what?
Janey shrugged. "In case the house burn down." She smiled then. "Or bad weather slop the roads so bad I can't get here early enough for them. Case late guests need serving or cleaning up after. Anything. Don't ask me what whitefolks need at night."

"They used to be good whitefolks."

"Oh, yeah. They good. Can't say they ain't good. I wouldn't trade them for another pair, tell you that." (p. 300)

While Janey admits that she would rather serve the Bodwins than any other whitefolks, her endorsement is hardly wholehearted. She understands the practical side of the matter (that the Bodwins treat her well enough), but that does not mean that they treat her (or other blacks) as equals. This point is dramatically underscored by the small figurine that sits on a shelf near the back door of the Bodwins' kitchen. The figure depicts a kneeling black boy, with coins loaded in his mouth that could be used "to pay for a delivery or some other small service." But his body is so contorted – "His head was thrown back farther than a head could go, his hands were shoved in his pockets. Bulging like moons, two eyes were all the face he had above the gaping red mouth" – that he might be reminiscent of a lynching victim. There is still one more damning detail: "Painted across the pedestal he knelt on were the words 'At Yo Service'" (p. 300). As Trudier Harris points out, this figure represents Sambo, a stereotypical image of a docile, happy, lazy black man eager to serve whites (1990, pp. 335–6). As such, the figure symbolizes all the misunderstandings and ignorance that even well-intentioned white do-gooders inflict on black people.

And yet, the novel does not entirely condemn the Bodwins. Readers know from a conversation between Paul D and Stamp Paid that Mr. Bodwin decides not to press any charges against Sethe for her attempted assault with the ice pick. Stamp, a voice to be trusted in the novel, tells Paul D that he is pleased but not surprised by Bodwin's decision:

He's somebody never turned us down. Steady as a rock. I tell you something, if she had got to him, it'd be the worst thing in the world for us. You know, don't you, he's the main one kept Sethe from the gallows in the first place. (p. 312)

Even with his limits, Bodwin is a white man who can be counted on to help the black community, Stamp emphasizes.

It is also worth noting that Mr. Bodwin is one of the only white people in the novel to have his interior thoughts and memories streamed into the narrative voice. This interior view provides layers of complexity. Readers learn that Bodwin experienced abuse for his anti-slavery activism, being called a "bleached nigger" and having his face and hair blackened (p. 306). Yet readers might be suspicious of Bodwin's recalling the days of abolitionism as "stimulating," as though this were a time of high adventure without dire consequences. But as the narrative stream continues, readers also discover that Bodwin presently misses not the heady days of "letters, petitions, meetings, debates . . . rescue and downright sedition," but the toys he buried in the yard of 124 when he was a boy (p. 307). Do these childhood memories suggest a retreat from history and its legacy, the kind of retreat that is available only to a propertied white man? Philip M. Weinstein argues that Bodwin's thoughts about his toys from childhood reveal him to be a "white landowner who has the luxury of pleasure-laden memories and who remembers 124 as ancestral property rather than a life-and-death space that Sethe and her children hold to/almost tear apart" (p. 164). True enough, and yet Lori Askeland's reading of the novel calls attention to the fact that Bodwin's sense of loss and his own mortality haunt his innermost thoughts; for Askeland, Bodwin in the climactic scene is "a fragile being who must, after all, be saved by a girl, Denver" (p. 174). Clearly, even in the case of a minor or secondary character like Edward Bodwin, careful textual scrutiny and multiple levels of interpretation are possible, and necessary, for understanding his role in the novel.

Of all the relationships between blacks and whites in Morrison's novel, the most promising is found in Amy Denver's and Sethe's accidental and healing encounter, which Bernard Bell has described as the novel's "brightest ray of hope for black and white sisterhood" (p. 11). Why Amy Denver, a young white woman, would assist Sethe, a pregnant black woman obviously fleeing slavery, is a valuable question to ponder. As Nicole M. Coonradt points out, "by abetting an escaped slave, Amy places herself in danger of serious punishment, including imprisonment, under the

"Fugitive Slave Law of 1850" '; Coonradt also notes that Amy no doubt would have had the "opportunity to turn Sethe in to receive a reward" if she were so inclined (p. 180). Indeed, Sethe must sense this danger as well since, when Amy asks for her name, she makes something up and answers "Lu." But Sethe is desperately in need of help, so she has to trust Amy on some level. And Amy, who has decided to flee her indentured servitude, has something in common with Sethe: the desire for freedom. The novel raises some other intriguing connections between the women: both are orphans; both have mothers who have experienced sexual exploitation; both are starving; both are uneducated. In other words, both Amy Denver and Sethe understand what it is like to be among the have-nots and the unfree in a nation that promotes principles of freedom and equality in its founding documents.

As escapees on the lam, Amy and Sethe create a sisterly bond out of their common experiences as women. Amy sings Sethe a lullaby to soothe her pain, exemplifying a caring, nurturing side that Sethe as a mother shows her own children. Sethe reassures Amy when Amy can hardly express the possibility that the cruel boss Mr. Buddy might be her father, for as an enslaved black woman, Sethe has certainly seen a good deal of white men's sexual enslavement of women. But to what degree do these sisterly bonds transcend the entrenched racial differences of America in 1855? In *Black Reconstruction in America, 1860–1880*, W. E. B. Du Bois insightfully analyzes the forces that kept white and black workers from acting in solidarity with each other on shared economic and class interests. Du Bois accounts for this lack of solidarity in part because of the nonmaterial benefits of white privilege:

> It must be remembered that the white group of laborers, while they received a low wage, were compensated in part by a sort of public and psychological wage. They were given public deference and titles of courtesy because they were white. They were admitted freely with all classes of white people to public functions, public parks, and the best schools. (1939, p. 700)

Thus, in Du Bois's analysis, the benefits of white privilege outweigh the benefits of class solidarity that would cross the "color-line" (1903, p. 9). Given this historical context, readers might expect Amy Denver's access to white privilege to prevail over her feelings of female solidarity with Sethe, but that is not exactly the trajectory Morrison's novel traces. The novel complicates their relationship in instructive ways.

As Lucille Fultz describes it, "Amy's alternating stance between the role of a white woman and the role of a mutually dependent fugitive invites readers" collusion and critique" (p. 36). For instance, while Amy Denver does not turn Sethe in to slavecatchers, it is also obvious that she treats her with contempt at times, addressing Sethe as though she lacks basic intelligence. Her initial greeting of Sethe is rude and racist: "Look there. A nigger. If that don't beat all" (p. 38). Self-absorbed with her own need for food, Amy almost walks off and leaves an obviously suffering Sethe. Then she tells her about her quest to make it to Boston to get some velvet, especially "carmine" velvet; her self-centeredness is glaring, and it continues until she finally asks Sethe a contemptuous and dehumanizing question: "What you gonna do, just lay there and foal?" (p. 41). When Sethe tells her, "I can't get up from here," finally Amy offers to help, first by helping her find an abandoned lean-to to stay the night and second by encouraging Sethe to keep moving, even through she has to crawl on her knees.

The mixture of caring and contempt continues as Amy rubs Sethe's swollen, numb legs and feet, while uttering one of the most-quoted lines from the novel: "Anything dead coming back to life hurts" (p. 42). But just a moment later, Amy rudely interjects, "Whose baby that? . . . You don't even know" (p. 92). When Sethe remarks that her back hurts and Amy finds the bloody welts from the beating Sethe has had at the hands of schoolteacher's nephews, Amy both sympathizes and draws her distance. She tells Sethe, "Glad I ain't you" (p. 94), on the one hand, but on the other, she comforts her by telling her the welts form something beautiful:

It's a tree, Lu. A chokecherry tree. See, here's the trunk – it's red and split wide open, full of sap, and this here's the parting for the branches. You got a mighty lot of branches. Leaves, too, look like, and dern if these ain't blossoms. Tiny little cherry blossoms, just as white. Your back got a whole tree on it. In bloom. (p. 93)

Amy's description of Sethe's back, Linden Peach observes, "imaginatively transforms the pain and humiliation of slavery" (p. 121). Carol E. Henderson concurs, pointing out that "Amy Denver signifies the possibility of imagining the scars of slavery as something other than what the master had in mind" (p. 99). Indeed, 18 years later, when Sethe tells Paul D about her back, she refers to having a tree there, following Amy's words and poetic imagery, rather than immediately talking about the whipping. Also worth noting is that Amy, although she tells Sethe that she will be heading over to the Pike to make her way to Boston, decides to accompany Sethe to the Ohio River, and so she is there when Sethe reaches the river and her labor pains begin. Amy thoughtlessly scolds her, as though Sethe could control when and where she goes into labor: "What you doing that for?" Amy exclaims, adding derogatorily, "Ain't you got a brain in your head? Stop that right now. I said stop it, Lu. You the dumbest thing on this here earth" (p. 98). Nevertheless, Amy pulls while Sethe pushes, and so Denver emerges into the outside world with two sets of loving hands to welcome her, two women to coo over her.

While it seems simplistic to read Amy Denver's role in the novel as entirely heroic (Coonradt, for example, describes her as a "savior," as a "prophetic healer," and as a "biblical Good Samaritan" (pp. 176, 179)), Morrison's novel presents the connection between Amy and Sethe at Denver's birth as something worth pondering:

On a riverbank in the cool of a summer evening two women struggled under a shower of silvery blue. They never expected to see each other again in this world and at the moment couldn't care less. But there on a summer night surrounded by blue-fern they did something together appropriately and well. A pateroller passing would have sniggered to see two throw-away people, two lawless outlaws – a slave and a barefoot whitewoman with unpinned hair – wrapping a ten-minute-old baby in the rags they wore. But no pateroller came and no preacher. . . . There was nothing to disturb them at their work. So they did it appropriately and well. (pp. 99–100)

In this heightened lyrical language, the novel shows Sethe and Amy, a black woman and a white woman, stepping outside the social constraints of America in 1855 and doing something wondrous together: they birth Sethe's baby, and they bridge (momentarily, at least) the racial differences of their time and place. Naming her baby girl after Amy Denver, Sethe makes sure that this moment of bonding will be remembered. Furthermore, as Fultz suggests in her reading of this scene, the setting is significant: "At the site of Denver's birth – the Ohio River – the border between North and South, between freedom and enslavement, between life and death, the narrative holds out the promise that separation based on differences may be overcome" (p. 38).

One of the intertexts that stands closely behind the encounter between Amy Denver and Sethe in *Beloved* is Mark Twain's well-known 1885 novel, *Adventures of Huckleberry Finn*. When Amy initially stumbles upon Sethe, she is actually looking for huckleberries (p. 39). Like Huck, Amy is about 16 years old, and she is perhaps dangerously innocent enough to challenge the codes of slavery and racism unawares in her encounter with Sethe, as Huck does when he travels down the Mississippi River with Jim on a raft. Because of these connections and others, Richard C. Moreland has described Amy as "Twain's Huckleberry Finn in girlface" (p. 164). Careful readers will note other subtle allusions to Twain's canonical novel in *Beloved*: for instance, Sethe works for a restaurant owner named *Sawyer*, and can barely tolerate standing in line until all the white customers are helped at a store run by the *Phelps* family.

In *Playing in the Dark*, Morrison comments directly and provocatively on how Twain's famous novel reveals what she calls "the parasitical nature of white freedom" (1992b, p. 57). Morrison points out that, in the much-criticized and debated final section of Twain's novel, when Huck and Tom Sawyer launch their elaborate and sometimes cruel plot to free Jim:

the fatal ending becomes the elaborate deferment of a necessary and necessarily unfree Africanist character's escape, because freedom has no meaning to Huck or to the text without the specter of enslavement, the anodyne to individualism; the yardstick of absolute power over the life of another; the signed, marked, informing, and mutating presence of a black slave. (1992b, p. 56)

In striking ways, Morrison's remarks about the racial dynamics of Twain's novel describe how many of the white characters in *Beloved* measure their superiority and freedom – except for Amy Denver, that is. In *Beloved*, Morrison lays bare the operations of white supremacy and privilege in nineteenth-century America, but she also offers the glimmer of a black and white bond that arises not out of bondage, but out of mutual needs and desires. In Sethe's encounter with Amy Denver, Morrison rewrites the Huck–Jim relationship, showing that the desire for freedom, for a "livable life" (1987b, p. 234), need not be constructed by racial hierarchy and opposition where white freedom is measurable only against black unfreedom and subordination. While Fultz is quite right to point out that, once they go their separate ways, Amy's future prospects in Boston will certainly be brighter than Sethe's future as a fugitive in Ohio (p. 38), Morrison's novel emphasizes the unexpected bonding that occurs between the two women despite class and racial stratifications. Through Sethe's and Amy's encounter, Morrison's novel advances the hope that dreams of freedom might be shared and supported across entrenched lines of difference.

QUESTIONS FOR FURTHER ANALYSIS

1. As Mae G. Henderson points out, schoolteacher is a destructive force in *Beloved* not only as a slaveholder, but also as a scholar (p. 69): he serves as "a data-collector, cataloguer, classifier, and taxonomist concerned with matters of materiality and empiricism" (p. 70). His methods, Henderson insists, scientifically dis-member slaves, including their bodies and their humanity. How does Morrison's novel call into question schoolteacher's scholarly and scientific methods? To what degree are these methods complicit with white supremacy in

the novel? What alternative methods of knowing and knowledge production does the novel claim to re-member black people and black history on their own terms?

2. Avery F. Gordon insists that *Beloved* has a provocative message for white readers about the legacy of slavery and the continuing effects of white privilege:

> What Morrison is saying . . . is that if we listen carefully to the voices of 124, we will hear not only "their" story, the old story of the past, but how we are in this story, even now, even if we do not want to be. To be in the seemingly old story now scared and not wishing to be there but not having anywhere else you can go that feels like a place you can belong is to be haunted. . . . Reckoning with ghosts is not like deciding to read a book: you cannot simply choose the ghosts with which you are willing to engage. . . . Though you can repeat over and over again, as if the incantation were a magic that really worked, I am not Schoolteacher / He is not me, the ghostly matter will not go away. It is waiting for you and it will shadow you and it will outwit all your smart moves. (p. 190)

For Gordon, the reader's consciousness of being haunted may lead to significant epistemological and ethical insights, since it involves being caught up in history and its effects, by the recognition that all truths are partial and relational, and by an awareness of one's own potential complicity. How does Morrison's novel achieve this effect of haunting readers? Does the novel create different kinds of haunting for white readers and black readers?

THROUGH THE CHARACTERS TO THE KEY THEMES AND ISSUES

In a 1983 interview with Nellie McKay, Toni Morrison expansively describes her goals as a writer in building characters and representing the lives of African Americans. "The people in these novels are complex," Morrison explains:

> Some are good and some are bad, but most of them are bits of both. I try to burrow as deeply as I can into characters. . . . It seems to me that one of the most fetching qualities of black people is the variety in which they come, and the enormous layers of lives that they live. It is a compelling thing for me because no single layer is "it". (1983, p. 145)

Indeed, the preceding chapters trace Morrison's extraordinary ability to make the lives, struggles, and dreams of her characters come alive in *Beloved* in richly textured layers. As Morrison says, "no single layer is 'it'," no character is completely good or bad. She cautions her readers not to oversimplify, to be prepared to see a character like Sethe, for example, as heroic, naïve, rash, strong, loving, murderous, all-sacrificing, completely absorbed in her own explanations, and more. The same plethora of qualities – a dynamic mixture of weaknesses and virtues – can be found in all the black characters of *Beloved*, and in most of the white characters as well (with the notable exception of schoolteacher).

It is common critical practice for the analysis of character in literature to involve several levels of investigation: examining the character's words and actions; examining what other characters say about him or her; and examining what the narrative voice reveals about the character. All of these methods are necessary for understanding Morrison's characters, but a full analysis of Sethe, Baby Suggs, Paul D, Beloved, Stamp Paid, and the other compelling characters of *Beloved* also requires the ability to parse what is not being said or shown directly. Grappling with the characters of *Beloved* offers keen insights into narrative point of view – especially concerning what characters say aloud, what they think to themselves, and what desires and conflicts they may experience at a subconscious level – but Morrison's narrative stream of consciousness makes some things available only to the reader. For instance, it is useful to look back to identify what Sethe says to Beloved directly versus what she thinks to herself, or what she ponders so deeply that she is not even aware of her own thought-flow. Or consider the traumatic experience of Paul D in the Alfred, Georgia, prison camp: are Morrison's readers the only ones privy to his story? Morrison's ability to render character from the inside out, through layers of interiority, significantly endows the lives of her black characters with an eloquence, musicality, and intelligence that went unrecorded in the official discourses of the slave era. Furthermore, the complex layers of interiority in Morrison's characters lead to important epistemological and ethical insights about one person's capacity to know another person fully, and about anyone's ability to recognize and articulate the deepest desires, fears, and dreams of his or her innermost self.

It is also important, when analyzing the characters of *Beloved*, to bear in mind that the novel questions many of the premises underlying autonomous, bourgeois individualism. In her book-length study of Morrison's novels, Gurleen Grewal underscores this point:

> Morrison pays a great deal of attention to individual consciousness; we are made to see what constitutes a particular character's subjectivity and what diminishes or augments the humanity of that character. But in that appraisal Morrison compels us to evaluate not just the individual but the entire complex sociopolitical history that constitutes the individual. (p. 13)

Following Grewal's observation means that readers need to consider Morrison's characters as individuals, as members of a community, and as part of a collective struggle to gain recognition for minority peoples. No one stands or falls alone in *Beloved*; in Morrison's fictional world, black characters are anchored in community, or, when they are isolated, they long for connection and community. Moreover, on the question of individual agency, Morrison's novel follows a middle ground, carefully delineating historical conditions and social hierarchies that constrain her characters' ability to act or choose freely, as well as insisting that acts of resistance are possible and that the capacity to hold onto love and humanity under the most terrifying conditions is heroic.

Placing individual characters in social and historical context is precisely the methodology of this study. While key characters such as Baby Suggs, Stamp Paid, Sethe and Beloved, Denver, Paul D, Amy Denver, and others have been discussed as individuals, they have also been analyzed in relation to each other and in relation to the historical and social conditions that impinge upon them. The chapters of this book have outlined the novel's relation to history; its engagements with discourses of motherhood and manhood; its interest in trauma, the uncanny, and in representing the limits of what can be articulated; its interrogation of the meanings of race; and its critical examination of whiteness. This approach to character is demanding but ultimately rewarding.

As Valerie Smith has observed, "*Beloved* is a novel of such extraordinary plenitude that new meanings and ways of reading emerge whenever one repositions oneself as critic" (1990, p. 353). Analyzing the characters of *Beloved* involves a wide-ranging and sophisticated set of interpretive skills: the ability to scrutinize the text and to gather complicated, even contradictory evidence from it; a knowledge of historical context, related specifically to Margaret Garner and more broadly to slavery and reconstruction; the capacity to build intertextual connections between Morrison's other writing (essays, interviews, and novels) and the work of writers she was influenced by; an investigation into what Morrison scholars have said about *Beloved*; a familiarity with theories of subjectivity, identity, language, knowledge, power, desire, and so on; and a philosophical perspective that acknowledges and welcomes paradox, multiplicity, ambiguity, and undecidability. The previous chapters have shown that a combination of theoretical perspectives – historicism, black feminist theory, African American cultural studies, psychoanalytic theory, deconstruction, masculinity and queer studies, Marxism and whiteness studies – is crucial for coming to terms with Morrison's characters.

Even with all that has unfolded in the preceding pages, this guide to *Beloved*'s characters is designed not to be an end point, but rather to form a starting point for readers to follow their own perceptions and questions. At the end of *Beloved*, Paul D thinks to himself, "He wants to put his story next to hers" (p. 322), signaling his renewed commitment to Sethe, on one level, but also acknowledging that one person's story needs another's (and still others) to begin to speak truly and richly about black life in all its diversity. His self-reflection might be seen as an important directive for readers and students of the novel as well. Or, as Cheryl A. Wall puts it, readers of the novel "must make their own imaginative act": "Readers of *Beloved* are invited to do so through listening to a chorus of voices and responding to their call. Their call entreats readers to be open to the awe and reverence and mystery and magic that the novel inscribes" (p. 115).

Readers who answer the call and who engage in the multilayered kinds of analysis suggested here will find themselves immersed in the rich thematics and probing philosophical questions of Morrison's novel: Is freedom a matter of legal statute, a physical state, or a psychological condition? How might freedom be rethought so that it does not depend on slavery as an opposition to define itself? Is a selfless love of others the greatest virtue for women, or the greatest danger? When is love "too thick" (p. 193), and when is it too "thin" (p. 194)? Is it safer not to love at all, and if so, is that safety worth having? What inhibits and what releases memory? Are there experiences that might be best forgotten or unspoken? What is the critical difference between "a loneliness that can be rocked" and "a loneliness that roams" (p. 323), and can either be assuaged? Is it possible in any substantial way to work through traumas that are unspeakable or unspoken? Or does trauma signify something that is beyond reparation or articulation? How can the lives of black people under slavery be written in such a way as to acknowledge devastating cruelty *and* creative resistance? What is a "real" man: someone who can endure torture and terror without breaking, or someone who honestly admits that his own concept of manhood is fragile? How might black men and black women come together without reproducing traditional gender expectations and hierarchies? Is it possible for whitefolks and black people to begin a dialogue that does not incorporate elements of white supremacy? These questions, and others, haunt the pages of *Beloved*.

Beloved also launches a critical engagement with the possibility of thinking beyond the determinations of race, a thematic that Morrison develops further in the subsequent novels of her trilogy. *Beloved* is set in the era of slavery, emancipation, and reconstruction in the U.S.A.; it unfolds, in other words, in a historical epoch in which race affected absolutely everything, even determining one's status as person or property. In the other two novels of her historical trilogy, Morrison has located later historical eras and opportunities to think beyond the racist determinations of slavery. In *Jazz*, the migration of her main characters from South to North allows them to transform themselves into what Alain Locke called the "New Negro" (p. 3). The language of jazz/*Jazz* also opens up improvisational and creative possibilities for refiguring the self. *Paradise* begins with a moment of shocking violence and a provocative sentence – "They shoot the white girl first" (1998, p. 3) – but then the race of the individual women living in the Convent is deliberately never identified in the course of the novel. One of the strongest themes that emerges in *Paradise* is the possibility of creating or imagining a diverse community that is not based on nationalist or racial exclusions. Indeed, in an essay titled "Home" that Morrison was working on as she was writing *Paradise*, Morrison talks about her responsibility as "an already- and always-raced writer" to "convert a racist house into a race-specific yet nonracist home" (1997, pp. 4, 5). Her most recent novels explore this complicated engagement with race in such a way as to reconstruct the house of race, to create new intellectual homes, safe social spaces, where race can be reimagined "without dominance – without hierarchy" (1997, p. 11).

Beloved starts readers on a journey that is threaded through Morrison's most recent novels, a journey that asks readers to reconsider fundamental assumptions about race, class, and gender, what makes a life "livable" (p. 234) or "unlivable" (p. 204), questions about freedom and bondage, as well as moral ambiguities and ethical responsibilities. It is important to recognize that these are not issues confined to the nineteenth century of Morrison's novel: they are issues clamoring for urgent attention in the contemporary world. Linden Peach highlights the timeliness of *Beloved* in his book on Morrison:

> Although set in the nineteenth century, *Beloved* has numerous implications for both black and white cultural identity in the twentieth century: the need for contemporary America to reclaim the full narrative of slavery, especially the suffering of black women; the need for white America to understand how slavery was justified as an intellectual and scientific project that failed to recognize the human cost; and the need for all potentially dominant cultures to appreciate that the brutality and racialism of slavery has extended far beyond the emancipation of slaves in the nineteenth century into contemporary America. (pp. 124–5)

Beloved, then, not only provides a vivid look inside the hearts, minds, and souls of African Americans in nineteenth-century America; it also serves as a critical guide for reimagining the world we live in today, a world in which difference and otherness matter all too much, in ways that too often lead to violence. Morrison's novel calls out to readers to begin the necessary work of drawing these connections.

GUIDE TO FURTHER READING

The annotated list of works that follows provides avenues for further research about *Beloved* as a novel and its connections to Morrison's other works.

Andrews, William L., and Nellie Y. McKay (eds) (1999) *Toni Morrison's "Beloved": A Casebook*. New York: Oxford University Press.
This collection provides important resources for analyzing *Beloved* in depth. It reprints two nineteenth-century texts about Margaret Garner, brings together seven important scholarly essays on *Beloved*, and includes an interview with Toni Morrison conducted by acclaimed black feminist scholars Nellie Y. McKay, Deborah McDowell, and Barbara Christian.

Beaulieu, Elizabeth Ann (ed.) (2003) *The Toni Morrison Encyclopedia*. Westport, CT: Greenwood Press.
This volume includes entries for all of Morrison's novels published before 2003, major characters, and place names. It also includes information about writers who influenced Morrison as a writer, such as William Faulkner, Mark Twain, and Virginia Woolf. Other entries outline recurring themes and images in Morrison's work (family, history, home, hunger, masculinity, memory, motherhood, music, myth, race, recovery, and violence, for example). The section of entries grouped together under the heading "Approaches to Morrison's Work" may be especially useful for students, in outlining representative Ecocritical, Feminist/Black Feminist, Historical, Pedagogical, Postcolonial, Psychoanalytic, and Womanist readings of her novels.

Fultz, Lucille P. (2003) *Toni Morrison: Playing With Difference.* Urbana: University of Illinois Press.
Fultz's book discusses otherness in Morrison's novels from *The Bluest Eye* through to *Paradise.* Fultz pays particular attention to the complex layers and nuances created by Morrison's narrative and aesthetic strategies; these nuances and strategies allow Morrison to "play with difference" – that is, to examine critically ideas of otherness rooted in normative conceptions of race, gender, class, and other markers of difference. Fultz's analysis is especially helpful in identifying the ethical imperatives of Morrison's novels and in suggesting that Morrison's fiction elicits an ethics of responsibility in readers.

Harris, Trudier (1991) *Fiction and Folklore: The Novels of Toni Morrison.* Knoxville: University of Tennessee Press.
Harris examines the influence of African American folklore and oral traditions on the characters, themes, and form of Morrison's novels from *The Bluest Eye* to *Beloved.* She argues that Morrison "saturates" her novels with folklore, but also adds her own twist to the traditions, often in order to create new myths or to raise moral ambiguities.

Jacobs, Harriet A. (1997) *Incidents in the Life of a Slave Girl, Written by Herself,* ed. Jean Fagan Yellin. Cambridge, MA: Harvard University Press.
Jacobs's 1861 slave narrative is a compelling reading experience alongside *Beloved.* Like Sethe in Morrison's novel, Jacobs experiences the jubilation of having children even as she begins to recognize the terrors of motherhood under slavery, and also like Sethe, Jacobs finds ways to resist her white master. The literary discourse available to Jacobs in the nineteenth century to tell her story makes for a valuable comparison with Morrison's innovative approach to revealing what has been unspoken about slavery, especially for black women.

King, Lovalerie, and Lynn Orilla Scott (eds) (2006) *James Baldwin and Toni Morrison: Comparative Critical and Theoretical Essays.* New York: Palgrave Macmillan.
The 13 essays collected in this volume bring James Baldwin's

fiction and essays into dialogue with Toni Morrison's fiction and nonfiction, an important and valuable endeavor since Baldwin was a formative influence on Morrison. The selections by Michelle H. Phillips, Carol E. Henderson, Babacar M'Baye, E. Frances White, and Keith Mitchell are particularly useful for students analyzing *Beloved*.

Kolmerten, Carol A., Stephen M. Ross, and Judith B. Wittenberg (eds) (1997) *Unflinching Gaze: Morrison and Faulkner Re-Envisioned*. Jackson: University Press of Mississippi.
This collection includes 15 essays from noted scholars examining William Faulkner's and Toni Morrison's fiction together from the perspectives of influence, intertextuality, racial and gender difference, narrative strategies, and reworkings of myth and history. Morrison's *Beloved* is read productively alongside Faulkner's *As I Lay Dying*, *Requiem for a Nun*, and especially *Absalom, Absalom!*

Morrison, Toni (1992) *Playing in the Dark: Whiteness and the Literary Imagination*. Cambridge, MA: Harvard University Press.
In this study (originally delivered as the Massey Lectures at Harvard University), Morrison looks at how blackness (ideas of blackness, images of blackness, black characters, and so on) has structured canonical American literary texts by white authors. Morrison notes that "black slavery enriched the country's creative possibilities" for white writers, and coins the term "American Africanism" to describe "a fabricated brew of darkness, otherness, alarm, and desire" that is employed by such writers to define freedom, autonomy, authority, and innocence in connection to whiteness, and in opposition to blackness and slavery (p. 38). Morrison's readings of American Africanism in works by Willa Cather, Edgar Allan Poe, Mark Twain, and Ernest Hemingway are especially insightful.

O'Reilly, Andrea (2004) *Toni Morrison and Motherhood: A Politics of the Heart*. Albany: State University of New York Press.
O'Reilly traces the theme of "motherwork" in Morrison's fiction (through *Paradise*), which she defines as being "concerned with

how mothers, raising black children in a racist and sexist world, can best protect their children, instruct them in how to protect themselves, [and] challenge racism" (p. 1). Positioning Morrison "as a maternal theorist" (p. xi), this study devotes individual chapters to various forces that disrupt mothering and to those that restore maternal bonds and healing.

Peach, Linden (2000) *Toni Morrison* (2nd ed.). New York: St. Martin's.
Peach includes individual chapters on Morrison's first seven novels (up to *Paradise*), under the rubrics of "early novels," "romance novels," "the middle passage," and "the 1990s." The first chapter may be especially valuable to students as it outlines various biographical contexts and schools of interpretation that promote a complex understanding of Morrison's oeuvre.

Rigney, Barbara Hill (1991) *The Voices of Toni Morrison*. Columbus: Ohio State University Press.
Rigney examines how Morrison's fiction, from *The Bluest Eye* through *Beloved*, breaks with patriarchal and Western ways of knowing to voice a black feminine/feminist aesthetic and vision. Emphasizing Morrison's interest in redefining the lives of black women and men, Rigney's analysis employs French feminist theory – because of its focus on the feminine and gender, as well as its ability to articulate radical otherness – along with African American critical theory in order to underscore the complexities of race.

Solomon, Barbara H. (ed.) (1998) *Critical Essays on Toni Morrison's "Beloved"*. New York: G. K. Hall.
This collection includes a representative selection of reviews of *Beloved*, reprints 12 significant essays on the novel, publishes four new essays, and includes Morrison's commentary on the opening sentences of the novel (taken from Morrison's groundbreaking essay "Unspeakable Things Unspoken').

Taylor-Guthrie, Danille (ed.) (1994) *Conversations with Toni Morrison*. Jackson: University Press of Mississippi.
This volume collects 24 important interviews with Morrison dating from 1974 to 1992. The interviews provide valuable

insight into Morrison's development as a writer, and several of them include Morrison's comments on the process of writing *Beloved* specifically. The index to the volume makes it possible to trace major themes and references across various interviews and novels.

Toni Morrison: Profile of a Writer (1987), prod. and dir. Alan Benson; ed. Melvyn Bragg. London Weekend Television co-production with RM Arts. Home Vision, videocassette, 52 min.

This profile of Toni Morrison was prepared at about the same time as the release of *Beloved*, and Morrison discusses quite poignantly the problems she faced writing about slavery and the kind of research she conducted while working on the novel. Dramatic readings of excerpts from the novel by Guy Gregory and Bonnie Greer also provide insight into the lyricism and power of Morrison's language in key scenes.

Wall, Cheryl A. (2005) *Worrying the Line: Black Women Writers, Lineage, and Literary Tradition*. Chapel Hill: University of North Carolina Press.

The title of Wall's book, "worrying the line," comes from a blues trope. Wall extends this trope to contemporary black women's writing to bring to light the genealogical quest for "lineage" and "literary traditions" that recurs in these texts and to show how they locate other ways of knowing to fill in gaps in history and other official stories. Wall's study is valuable for discussing Morrison's *Beloved*, *Song of Solomon*, and *Sula*, and for placing Morrison's novels in relation to works by Audre Lorde, Gayl Jones, Alice Walker, Gloria Naylor, Paule Marshall, and other black women writers.

Weisenburger, Steven (1998) *Modern Medea: A Family Story of Slavery and Child-Murder From the Old South*. New York: Hill and Wang.

Weisenburger's book is the most carefully and thoroughly researched account of the historical Margaret Garner. It includes information about Margaret's life, both before, during, and after her escape from slavery and the killing of her daughter Mary. It also provides information about her white masters, the Gaines family, and covers in detail the inspired, but ultimately unsuccessful legal strategies of her defense team. The final section, which discusses how the Margaret Garner case became mythologized, will be of particular interest to readers of *Beloved.*

BIBLIOGRAPHY

Below is a list of all texts quoted from or referred to in the previous chapters, divided into separate categories for primary texts and secondary works.

PRIMARY TEXTS

Morrison, Toni (1970) *The Bluest Eye*. New York: Holt, Rinehart, and Winston.

—— (1973) *Sula*. New York: Knopf.

—— (1974) "Behind the making of *The Black Book*," *Black World* (February), pp. 86–90.

—— (1976) "A slow walk of trees (as grandmother would say), hopeless (as grandfather would say)," *New York Times Magazine* (4 July), pp. 104–5, 150ff.

—— (1977) *Song of Solomon*. New York: Knopf.

—— (1981) *Tar Baby*. New York: Knopf.

—— (1983) "An interview with Toni Morrison" [interview with Nellie McKay], reprinted in *Conversations with Toni Morrison*, ed. Danille Taylor-Guthrie. Jackson: University Press of Mississippi, 1994, pp. 138–55.

—— (1985) "A conversation" [interview with Gloria Naylor], reprinted in *Conversations with Toni Morrison*, ed. Danille Taylor-Guthrie. Jackson: University Press of Mississippi, 1994, pp. 188–217.

—— (1986) "An interview with Toni Morrison" [interview with Christina Davis], reprinted in *Conversations with Toni Morrison*, ed. Danille Taylor-Guthrie. Jackson: University Press of Mississippi, 1994, pp. 223–33.

—— (1987a) "The site of memory," in *Inventing the Truth: The Art and Craft of Memoir*, ed. William Zinsser. Boston, MA: Houghton Mifflin, pp. 101–24.

—— (1987b) *Beloved*. New York: Vintage International, 2004.

—— (1988) "In the realm of responsibility: a conversation with Toni Morrison" [interview with Marsha Darling], reprinted in *Conversations with Toni Morrison*, ed. Danille Taylor-Guthrie. Jackson: University Press of Mississippi, 1994, pp. 246–54.

—— (1989a) "A bench by the road," *The World: Journal of the Unitarian Universalist Association* (January/February), pp. 4–5, 37–41.

—— (1989b) "Unspeakable things unspoken: the Afro-American presence in American literature," *Michigan Quarterly Review*, 28, pp. 1–34.

—— (1989c) "The pain of being black: an interview with Toni Morrison" [interview with Bonnie Angelo], reprinted in *Conversations with Toni Morrison*, ed. Danille Taylor-Guthrie. Jackson: University Press of Mississippi, 1994, pp. 255–61.

—— (1989d), "A conversation with Toni Morrison" [interview with Bill Moyers], reprinted in *Conversations with Toni Morrison*, ed. Danille Taylor-Guthrie. Jackson: University Press of Mississippi, 1994, pp. 262–74.

—— (1992a) *Jazz*. New York: Knopf.

—— (1992b) *Playing in the Dark: Whiteness and the Literary Imagination*. Cambridge, MA: Harvard University Press.

—— (1993) "Nobel Lecture 1993." Online at www.nobelprize. org/nobel_prizes/literature/laureates/1993/morrison-lecture [accessed 14 May 2007].

—— (1997) "Home," in *The House That Race Built*, ed. Wahneema Lubiano. New York: Pantheon, pp. 3–12.

—— (1998) *Paradise*. New York: Knopf.

—— (2003) *Love*. New York: Knopf.

SECONDARY WORKS

Als, Hilton (2003) "Ghosts in the house," *New Yorker* (27 October), pp. 64–75.

Askeland, Lori (1992) "Remodeling the model home in *Uncle Tom's Cabin* and *Beloved*," reprinted in *Toni Morrison's "Beloved": A Casebook*, ed. William L. Andrews and Nellie Y. McKay. New York: Oxford University Press, 1999, pp. 159–78.

Atkinson, Yvonne (2000) "Language that bears witness: the black English oral tradition in the works of Toni Morrison," in *The Aesthetics of Toni Morrison: Speaking the Unspeakable*, ed. Marc C. Conner. Jackson: University Press of Mississippi, pp. 12–30.

Atwood, Margaret (1987) "Haunted by their nightmares," rev. of *Beloved* by Toni Morrison, reprinted in *Critical Essays on Toni Morrison's "Beloved"*, ed. Barbara H. Solomon. New York: G. K. Hall, 1998, pp. 39–42.

Baldwin, James (1998) *Collected Essays*. New York: Library of America.

Barnett, Pamela E. (1997) "Figurations of rape and the super-natural in *Beloved*," *PMLA*, 112, pp. 418–27.

Bell, Bernard W. (1992) "*Beloved*: a womanist neo-slave narrative; or multivocal remembrances of things past," *African American Review*, 26, pp. 7–15.

Beloved (1998) Dir. Jonathan Demme. Perf. Oprah Winfrey, Danny Glover, Thandie Newton. Touchstone Pictures, film, 172 min.

Bhabha, Homi K. (2004) *The Location of Culture* (rev. ed.). London: Routledge.

Bradfield, Scott (2004) "Why I hate Toni Morrison's *Beloved*," *Denver Quarterly*, 38, (4), pp. 86–99.

Brown, Rosellen (1987) "The pleasure of enchantment," rev. of *Beloved* by Toni Morrison, reprinted in *Critical Essays on Toni Morrison's "Beloved"*, ed. Barbara H. Solomon. New York: G. K. Hall, 1998, pp. 59–63.

Byatt, A. S. (1987) "An American masterpiece," rev. of *Beloved* by Toni Morrison, *Guardian* (16 October), p. 13.

Christian, Barbara (1990) "'Somebody forget to tell somebody something': African-American women's historical novels," in *Wild Women in the Whirlwind*, ed. Joanne M. Braxton and Andrée N. McLaughlin. New Brunswick, NJ: Rutgers University Press, pp. 326–41.

Clemons, Walter (1987) "A gravestone of memories," rev. of *Beloved* by Toni Morrison, *Newsweek* (28 September), pp. 74–5.

Coonradt, Nicole M. (2005) "To be loved: Amy Denver and human need – bridges to understanding in Toni Morrison's *Beloved*," *College Literature*, 32 (4), pp. 168–87.

Crouch, Stanley (1987) "Aunt Medea," rev. of *Beloved* by Toni Morrison, *New Republic* (19 October), pp. 38–43.

Cutter, Martha (2000) "The story must go on and on: the fantastic, narration, and intertextuality in Toni Morrison's *Beloved* and *Jazz*," *African American Review*, 34, pp. 61–75.

Davies, Carole Boyce (1991) "Mother right/write revisited: *Beloved* and *Dessa Rose* and the construction of motherhood in black women's fiction," in *Narrating Mothers: Theorizing Maternal Subjectivities*, ed. Brenda O. Daly and Maureen T. Reddy. Knoxville: University of Tennessee Press, pp. 44–57.

Demetrakopoulos, Stephanie A. (1992) "Maternal bonds as devourers of women's individuation in Toni Morrison's *Beloved*," *African American Review*, 26, pp. 51–9.

Du Bois, W. E. B. (1903) *The Souls of Black Folk*. New York: Dover, 1994.

——— (1935) *Black Reconstruction, 1860–1880*. New York: Harcourt, Brace and Company.

Duvall, John N. (2000) *The Identifying Fictions of Toni Morrison: Modernist Authenticity and Postmodern Blackness*. New York: Palgrave.

Edelman, Lee (1994) *Homographesis*. New York: Routledge.

Freud, Sigmund (1995) "The uncanny," trans. Alix Strachey, in *Psychological Writings and Letters*, ed. Sander L. Gilman. New York: Continuum, pp. 120–53.

Fultz, Lucille P. (2003) *Toni Morrison: Playing With Difference*. Urbana: University of Illinois Press.

Genovese, Eugene D. (1974) *Roll, Jordan, Roll: The World the Slaves Made*. New York: Pantheon-Random House.

Gordon, Avery F. (1997) *Ghostly Matters: Haunting and the Sociological Imagination*. Minneapolis: University of Minnesota Press.

Grewal, Gurleen (1998) *Circles of Sorrow, Lines of Struggle: The Novels of Toni Morrison*. Baton Rouge: Louisiana State University Press.

Harris, Middleton (ed.) (1974) *The Black Book*. New York: Random House.

Harris, Trudier (1990) "Escaping slavery but not its images," in *Toni Morrison: Critical Perspectives Past and Present*, ed. Henry Louis Gates, Jr., and K. A. Appiah. New York: Amistad, 1993, pp. 330–41.

—— (1991) *Fiction and Folklore: The Novels of Toni Morrison*. Knoxville: University of Tennessee Press.

Henderson, Carol E. (2002) *Scarring the Black Body: Race and Representation in African American Literature*. Columbia: University of Missouri Press.

Henderson, Mae G. (1991) "Toni Morrison's *Beloved*: remembering the body as historical text," in *Comparative American Identities: Race, Sex, and Nationality in the Modern Text*, ed. Hortense J. Spillers. New York: Routledge, pp. 62–86.

Hill Collins, Patricia (2000) *Black Feminist Thought: Knowledge, Consciousness, and the Politics of Empowerment* (2nd ed.). New York: Routledge.

Holloway, Karla F. C. (1990) "*Beloved*: a spiritual," *Callaloo*, 13, pp. 516–25.

Horvitz, Deborah (1989) "Nameless ghosts: possession and dispossession in *Beloved*," *Studies in American Fiction*, 17 (2), pp. 157–67.

House, Elizabeth (1990) "Toni Morrison's ghost: the beloved who is not beloved," *Studies in American Fiction*, 18 (1), pp. 17–26.

Iannone, Carol (1987) "Toni Morrison's career," *Commentary* (December), pp. 59–63.

Jacobs, Harriet A. (1987) *Incidents in the Life of a Slave Girl, Written by Herself*, ed. Jean Fagan Yellin. Cambridge, MA: Harvard University Press.

James, Stanlie M. (1993) "Mothering: a possible black feminist link to social transformation?," in *Theorizing Black Feminism:*

The Visionary Pragmatism of Black Women, ed. Stanlie M. James and Abena P. A. Busia. London: Routledge, pp. 44–54.

Jordan, June, and Houston A. Baker Jr., *et al.* (1988) "Black writers in praise of Toni Morrison," *New York Times Book Review* (24 January). Online at www.nytimes.com/books/98/ 01/11/home/15084 [accessed 22 May 2007].

Keenan, Sally (1993) "'Four hundred years of silence': myth, history, and motherhood in Toni Morrison's *Beloved*," in *Recasting the World: Writing after Colonialism*, ed. Jonathan White. Baltimore, MD: Johns Hopkins University Press, pp. 45–81.

Krumholz, Linda (1992) "The ghosts of slavery: historical recovery in Toni Morrison's *Beloved*", reprinted in *Toni Morrison's "Beloved": A Casebook*, ed. William L. Andrews and Nellie Y McKay. New York: Oxford University Press, 1999, pp. 107–25.

Lidinksky, April (1994) "Prophesying bodies: calling for a politics of collectivity in Toni Morrison's *Beloved*," in *The Discourse of Slavery: Aphra Behn to Toni Morrison*, ed. Carl Plasa and Betty J. Ring. London: Routledge, pp. 191–216.

Locke, Alain (1925) "The new Negro," in *The New Negro, An Interpretation*, ed. Alain Locke. New York: Albert and Charles Boni, Inc., pp. 3–16.

M'Baye, Babacar (2006) "Resistance against racial, sexual, and social oppression in *Go Tell It on the Mountain* and *Beloved*," in *James Baldwin and Toni Morrison: Comparative Critical and Theoretical Essays*, ed. Lovalerie King and Lynn Orilla Scott. New York: Palgrave Macmillan, pp. 167–86.

Mobley, Marilyn Sanders (1988) "A different remembering: memory, history, and meaning in *Beloved*," in *Toni Morrison: Critical Perspectives Past and Present*, ed. Henry Louis Gates, Jr., and K. A. Appiah. New York: Amistad, 1993, pp. 356–65.

Moreland, Richard C. (1994) "'He wants to put his story next to hers': putting Twain's story next to hers in Morrison's *Beloved*," in *Toni Morrison: Critical and Theoretical Approaches*, ed. Nancy J. Peterson. Baltimore, MD: Johns Hopkins University Press, 1997, pp. 155–79.

Nelson, Jill (1998), "No more Mr. Nice Guy?" [profile of Denzel Washington]. *USA Weekend Magazine* (9–11 January). Online at www.usaweekend.com/98_issues/980109/980109denzel_ washington [accessed 30 April 2007].

O'Reilly, Andrea (2004) *Toni Morrison and Motherhood: A Politics of the Heart*. Albany: State University of New York Press.

Peach, Linden (2000) *Toni Morrison* (2nd ed.). New York: St. Martin's.

Rigney, Barbara Hill (1991) *The Voices of Toni Morrison*. Columbus: Ohio State University Press.

Rushdy, Ashraf H. A. (1992) "Daughters signifyin(g) history: the example of Toni Morrison's *Beloved*," *American Literature*, 64, pp. 567–97.

Schapiro, Barbara (1991) "The bonds of love and the boundaries of self in Toni Morrison's *Beloved*," *Contemporary Literature*, 32, pp. 194–210.

Scott, A. O. (2006) "In search of the best," *New York Times Book Review* (21 May). Online at www.movies 2.nytimes.com/2006/ 05/21/books/review/scott-essay [accessed 15 May 2007].

Sitter, Deborah Ayer (1992) "The making of a man: dialogic meaning in *Beloved*," *African American Review*, 26, pp. 17–29.

Smith, Valerie (1987) *Self-Discovery and Authority in Afro-American Narrative*. Cambridge, MA: Harvard University Press.

—— (1990) "'Circling the subject': history and narrative in *Beloved*," in *Toni Morrison: Critical Perspectives Past and Present*, ed. Henry Louis Gates, Jr., and K. A. Appiah. New York: Amistad, 1993, pp. 342–55.

Snitow, Ann (1987) "Death duties: Toni Morrison looks back in sorrow," rev. of *Beloved* by Toni Morrison, reprinted in *Critical Essays on Toni Morrison's "Beloved"*, ed. Barbara H. Solomon. New York: G. K. Hall, 1998, pp. 47–52.

Spillers, Hortense (1987) "Mama's baby, papa's maybe: an American grammar book," *Diacritics*, 17 (2), pp. 65–81.

Streitfeld, David (1993) "Author Toni Morrison wins Nobel Prize," *Washington Post* (8 October), pp. A1, A16.

Swedish Academy (1993) Press release for the Nobel Prize in Literature 1993 (7 October). Online at www.nobelprize.org/ nobel_prizes/literature/laureates/1993/press [accessed 14 May 2007].

Thurman, Judith (1987) "A house divided," rev. of *Beloved* by Toni Morrison, *New Yorker* (2 November), pp. 175–80.

Twain, Mark (2001) *Adventures of Huckleberry Finn* (Mark Twain Library). Berkeley: University of California Press.

Van Der Zee, James (photography), with Owen Dodson (poetry), and Camille Billops (text) (1978) *The Harlem Book of the Dead*. Dobbs Ferry, NY: Morgan and Morgan.

Wall, Cheryl A. (2005) *Worrying the Line: Black Women Writers, Lineage, and Literary Tradition*. Chapel Hill: University of North Carolina Press.

Weinstein, Philip M. (1996) *What Else But Love? The Ordeal of Race in Faulkner and Morrison*. New York: Columbia University Press.

Weisenburger, Steven (1998) *Modern Medea: A Family Story of Slavery and Child-Murder From the Old South*. New York: Hill and Wang.

Wyatt, Jean (1993) "Giving body to the word: the maternal symbolic in Toni Morrison's *Beloved*," *PMLA*, 108, pp. 474–88.

INDEX

AUG 2 3 2019

CPSIA information can be obtained
at www.ICGtesting.com
Printed in the USA
LVHW080440090819
627064LV00006B/141/P